'Although retirement is a transition commonly experienced by people as they reach the end of a work cycle, it is nevertheless a highly individualized experience. For many, it can also be the start of new beginnings. *Retiring Lives* gives a wonderful insight into the personal reflective process that retirement involves and allows readers to reflect in a meaningful way on their own retirement experience.'

**Tatiana Schifferle-Rowson, Social Gerontologist, University of Keele**

'With the added years of health and vitality that have been visited upon a new generation of retirees, we/they are in uncharted territory, entering a stage of life not seen before in human history. Many of us are wondering how we'll live, what we'll do, who we'll be for the next twenty or thirty years. This is a tremendous challenge and a tremendous opportunity – surely easier for some than for others. The authors of this book show the many ways that some retired professionals are moving through the transition in human terms and with the support of a group of kindred spirits. Some feel joyful at the freedom and chafe at the disbelieving tone of social conversations, while others take a longer time to adjust and find new networks and friends: "a steep learning curve", according to one. Stories are laced with sudden illness or the death of a spouse – "whatever our best laid plans … illness can upset everything at any time." Most are adept at reflecting on the experience and finding undiscovered strengths and sensations. The book is a worthy read for anyone thinking about retiring.'

**Jacquelyn B. James, Ph.D., Co-director of Research,**
**Sloan Center on Aging and Work/Workplace Flexibility;**
**Research Professor, Lynch School of Education,**
**Boston College, USA**

'This book provides a wide range of insights into patterns of life and how these are influenced by and shape the transition into retirement. The honest life stories, presented by the chapter authors, provide a clear picture of the thoughts and feelings being faced by people, especially professional women, as retirement is contemplated and experienced. The introduction grasps the diverse aspects of retirement planning and the range of chapters adds quality and depth to this helpful book. *Retiring Lives* will be helpful to anybody considering pre-retirement planning, for individuals themselves and for course providers. The 'live cases' add richness a˙ ˙ ˙ ˙ ˙ planning for retirement.'

**Anthony Chiva, Head of Education and Training, Li**

D1473470

# Retiring Lives

# Retiring Lives

Edited by Eileen Carnell and
Caroline Lodge

First published in 2009 by the Institute of Education, University of London,
20 Bedford Way, London WC1H 0AL
www.ioe.ac.uk/publications

© Institute of Education, University of London 2009

**British Library Cataloguing in Publication Data:**
A catalogue record for this publication is available from the British Library

ISBN 978 0 85473 848 9

Typeset in the United Kingdom by Hobbs the Printers Ltd, Totton, Hampshire, SO40 3WX
Printed by Elanders

# Contents

# Contributors

**Gillian Bennet** taught Art in secondary schools and retired from a deputy head's post at 50 following health problems. She makes studio pottery in her studio in North London, has travelled widely in Asia and Central America and spends time with her children, stepchildren and six grandchildren.

**Eileen Carnell** has been involved in teaching, professional development and educational research throughout her career. She has contributed to a range of publications and her most recent co-authored book *Passion and Politics* focuses on academic writing. It was published by the Institute of Education in 2008. Eileen is still enjoying paid work, now on a very part-time basis and a range of joyous activities. With her partner, Isobel, she lives in London and increasingly in Dorset by the sea.

**Marianne Coleman** has spent her working life in education and retired recently from her post as Reader in Educational Leadership and Management at the Institute of Education. She is currently working on funded short-term research projects as part of her plan for phased retirement and enjoying more time with her family, in particular, two baby grandsons.

**Jennifer Evans** worked for 25 years as a researcher and lecturer in education policy, mainly at the Institute of Education, but also at NFER and the House of Commons. In retirement she is enjoying looking after grandchildren and growing vegetables.

**Anne Freeman** taught in London schools for 30 plus years, the last ten years as head of a Design and Technology faculty. She now lives in Surrey and spends lots of time in her garden working, reading and relaxing.

**Lorna Hoey** has been a teacher of Art and English for over 30 years, teaching in Northern Ireland, Switzerland and London. Her new ambition is to become a published author of fiction for older teenagers. Apart from writing, her interests include painting, model-making, travelling and feeding the fox at the back door.

**Anne Gold** has just retired (almost) from 20 years of teaching in inner London comprehensive schools followed by 20 years of working as an academic at the Institute of Education, University of London. She has retired so recently that she hasn't really developed a rhythm of regular interests. She is having a good time, though – rather like a child in a sweetshop with almost too many exciting things to choose from.

**Ashley Kent** has recently retired as Professor of Geography Education at the Institute of Education – the culmination of a lifetime as a geography teacher! He is now adjusting to – and so far enjoying – a quite different, yet equally full life.

**Alison Kirton** has 40 years experience of teaching Social Science and Humanities in different institutions in the UK and abroad. Since 1991 she has managed the PGCE in Social Science at the Institute of Education. Her main commitment has been curriculum innovation designed to provide better educational opportunities for female, working-class and ethnic minority students, using, wherever possible, active pedagogies with an empowering and democratic aim. She is now retired and lives in France.

**Diana Leonard** started work as a science teacher, but undertook a PhD in anthropology and ended up teaching sociology and then women's studies at the Institute of Education. She has been there for many years and is still unwilling to tear herself away: she continues happily as an emeritus professor. But much more of her time can now be devoted to gardening, family and holidays.

**Caroline Lodge** has worked all her adult life in education, pausing only to gain a daughter and an MA. At 60 she is a member of the Retiring Women group as she retires slowly from her position as a lecturer in education into an unknown future that involves a new grandson.

**Jacqui MacDonald** is a qualified teacher and a trained Careers Education and Guidance specialist and has worked in higher education as a lecturer and consultant for the last 17 years. She currently works as head of Staff Development at the Institute of Education, University of London, and is the chair of the Bloomsbury Colleges staff development forum. She is a trained mentor and coach and works on a voluntary basis for the Prince's Trust as a business mentor. She is a Justice of the Peace.

**Ted Mercer** was a primary headteacher in the ILEA (Inner London Education Authority). He became an inspector before retiring at 65, but he continued to work in a part-time consultancy role for a few years after retiring.

**Alex Moore** has worked as a schoolteacher and university lecturer since 1969. An emeritus professor at the Institute of Education, he now divides most of his time between writing, teaching, travelling the globe and enjoying his rapidly expanding family.

**Barbara Patilla** retired this year, aged 61, after working all her adult life. For the last 28 years she has taught in secondary schools in Tower Hamlets apart from three years working as an advisory teacher in the ILEA. She also has experience of teaching English in Indonesia and working for a pharmaceutical company.

**Anne Peters** has now retired for five years, having been head of Information and Services at the Institute of Education. She now does lots of voluntary work, as a trustee and supporting individuals in difficulties.

**Sid Reddy** came into Financial Advice after a career in teaching and retail management. He currently works as an Independent Financial Adviser and also advises charitable organisations on various aspects of Financial Planning. He works largely from home so he can work times suited to himself and spend time with his family.

# Acknowledgements

First we would like to thank the members of the Retiring Women group who were the inspiration for this book. We would like to thank each of them for their individual stories and all the other authors for their wonderful contributions to this publication.

We would like to say a big thank you to Robert Taylor, the photographer. Robert was a joy to work with on this project. And we think his portraits bring the book to life.

We are grateful to Jacqui MacDonald and Staff Development at the Institute of Education, University of London, for supporting the Retiring Women group.

Several workshops have been organised by Staff Development for staff considering retiring and we would like to thank all the people who attended these workshops for comments and reactions to draft chapters.

The reviewers made many helpful suggestions to which we have tried to respond to make this book more helpful to the readers.

We are also grateful to the production team: in particular to Jim Collins who assisted the publication with good humour, patience and constructive comments and also to Sally Sigmund, Nicole Gyulay, Daniel Sinclair and Liz Dawn.

The editors, contributors and publisher would like to thank the following for kind permission to reproduce the following copyright material.

'One Art' from *The Complete Poems 1927–1979* by Elizabeth Bishop. Copyright © 1979, 1983 by Alice Helen Methfessel. Reprinted by permission of Farrar, Straus and Giroux, LLC.

'Lines on Retirement, after Reading Lear' by David Wright. Originally published in *In a Fine Frenzy: Poets Respond to Shakespeare* by David Starkey and Paul J. Willis (eds) (University of Iowa Press, 2005).

'Teacher's Christmas' by U.A. Fanthorpe. Originally published in *A Watching Brief* (Peterloo Poets, 1987).

'Elizabeth's boureki' by Elizabeth Cradick. Originally published in *Cretan Village Cooking. Traditional recipes from the taverna* Τα Απτερα (2006).

'Warning'. Copyright © Jenny Joseph, SELECTED POEMS, Bloodaxe 1992. Reproduced with permission of Johnson & Alcock Ltd.

# Introduction

## Eileen Carnell and Caroline Lodge

This book has been written for people who are considering retiring by people who have been thinking about and making changes towards retiring. People approach retiring in many different ways: some delay thinking about it, reluctant or unclear about the changes involved; some respond enthusiastically to the prospect; others may be filled with dread, with uncertainty, ambivalence, planfulness or any combination of the above. This book, *Retiring Lives*, is intended for purposeful readers who are thinking (or wanting to think) about retiring, and who want to read about the experiences of others to help them with their plans. While the contributors to this book all come from education, higher education and the schools' sector, we expect it to appeal to a wider range of readers – those who want to think about what retiring might mean to them, and about their choices in retiring.

Our title, *Retiring Lives*, is intended to indicate a focus on the process of retiring rather than the event of retirement or the period of one's life that is called retirement. All the stories indicate that retiring is a dynamic process, not a one-off event, and this important concept is central to the book's rationale. The title reflects the fluid and flexible nature of retiring as the narratives show. We have learned that retiring can be a lengthy process – a dynamic period in which retirees go through a series of transitions. This book captures many aspects of the process of retiring. The discussions focus on what 'retiring' and 'retirement' mean. The different metaphors and images (such as going into an airlock, going over a cliff) that are used by the writers capture some of these differing meanings. We also consider these in Chapter 1.

Our book is different from others in the field of ageing, gerontology or the sociology of retirement, in that it presents real accounts and from a range of perspectives that we hope will help readers in their decisions about retiring. This book demonstrates that no two stories are similar. There are some overarching themes that we discuss in Chapter 1 but the individual narratives are very different. The material also reflects people's experiences at various stages: some retired several years ago; some are still working, but only part-time.

Many of our contributors have chosen to retire gradually. Others have taken a decision to cease paid employment completely at one moment. This decision has been a particularly important one for the writers. Nor have we neglected what our colleague refers to as 'the dark side' of retiring, although most of the stories here are positive and upbeat. We suggest that being thoughtful and reflective about what retiring means to them has helped them.

## The particular qualities of the book – the stories

We have several reasons for collecting and examining these stories. First, we anticipate that the book will stir readers to think about their own retiring and help them in their own planning processes. We expect that readers will hold up these experiences against their own, learn from comparisons and similarities and have their thinking extended by doing this.

Second, the narratives provide rich and varied responses to the transitions of retiring. This is because they bring together many different aspects of the experiences of retiring: the social, psychological and practical. Together, the stories highlight many interrelated and overlapping dimensions. They provide an experiential dimension that goes beyond conventional, qualitative accounts.

Third, we have provided in the next chapter an analysis that will be interesting, useful and inspiring to both individual readers and retiring groups. We analyse the main themes that emerge across the narratives, including the factors that might be taken into account in making the decision to retire, leaving an organisation and marking the occasion, preparing and making plans, making sense of the transitions, finding support, noting the different dimensions of retiring lives, the interrelationship between retiring and getting older, thinking about bereavement and death, thinking about what retiring successfully might mean and being aware of this specific moment in time.

Fourth, the way the Retiring Women group functions (see Chapter 3) is extremely important in our lives because of the positive benefits that accrue from sharing experiences and the support that is offered. This book seeks to extend these functions by offering insights and understandings to the readers from the group as well as to others.

So we hope that the book will provide a stimulating and useful account for those considering retiring or changing how they view their working lives.

## What this book does not consider

The range of issues covered is not exhaustive. The contributors have all worked in the field of education and do not face serious financial or learning difficulties (see Notes on contributors). Neither do their stories dwell on mental health issues, although some of the group have survived periods of severe anxiety, panic attacks or depression leading up to and during retiring or post-retirement. We do not cover a wide spectrum of cultural, religious or ethnic issues. Although the original idea for this book came from a group of women, we have focused more on the various experiences of retiring than on gender issues in retiring. Some aspects of retiring, as of life, are gender-specific, but it is not the purpose of this book to offer an extended exploration of these.

Nor is this book a manual on retiring. It has been suggested to us that we might take a more instrumental stance but, as we hinted at earlier, we would like the reader to engage in personal reflection as they read. However, for those who want to engage directly with material in the book we have included a chapter on retiring as an aspect of professional development (see Chapter 16). Readers will find specific activities that address key questions in relation to their own circumstances, such as developing a vision of life as a retired person, drawing up a retiring plan, keeping reflective accounts, noting feelings, worries and hopes about retiring and so on. We have not integrated these into the book but readers may wish to make notes around these suggested activities as they read through the different chapters of the book.

## The organisation of *Retiring Lives*

The book is divided into three sections. Following this introduction, Section 1, *Big issues and the experience of the Retiring Women group*, offers an overall analysis of themes from the stories, and it describes the setting up of the Retiring Women group and the lessons that we have learned from running it. This is intended to be useful to others, women and men, who wish to get a group together or for groups that already exist. There has been a lot of interest in what we do so we are aware that many others can see the value of sharing experiences. One way to share experiences and feelings is through a group, another way is through this book. We hope the review of our group's learning and the stories of its members, and others, will be helpful.

The fourteen personal narratives form the heart of the book. Section 2, *Retiring stories*, presents many different stories from men and women who have considered retiring and are at various stages in the process, ranging from still being employed on a part-time basis to being fully retired for several years. When we began to write the book we thought it would consist of the stories of the eight members of the Retiring Women group but after many conversations we decided to widen the book's content to include men and people from a number of different organisations. We are so glad that we made this decision as their accounts provide very rich and varied contributions.

Section 3, *Supporting and celebrating retiring*, considers some very practical matters. One chapter on retiring as an aspect of professional development provides a set of reflective activities which will be useful for individuals or groups to consider; recurring financial themes are the subject of another piece; a further chapter examines many reasons to be cheerful – a list of many of the benefits, allowances and privileges of becoming older.

In the Appendix we have included an annotated bibliography identifying novels, poetry, books on transitions, health and other relevant resources that the Retiring Women group members have found extremely helpful, informative and amusing. The focus is around different perspectives of retiring and ageing. This is a fairly random selection that we have shared and discussed. It is therefore not a comprehensive or representative selection.

Throughout the book we have included poems and gobbets that we have also passed around the group. We like these and hope you will too.

We enjoyed the process of editing *Retiring Lives*. We read and reread the stories many times and talked about them to draw out the main themes for Chapter 1. This chapter was written together, and then circulated in draft form to all the contributors, and their insights and comments helped us become clearer about some issues. We also discussed many of the emergent themes at our monthly meetings of the Retiring Women group and used this chapter as a focus of discussion in the Retiring Workshops that we were running as part of the staff development programme for other staff in our organisation. Reading these stories has helped us understand the issues at a more fundamental level and consider how these relate to our own lives. We hope that, in the same way, the many stories and other contents of the book will help readers make sense of their own experiences of retiring.

## Section 1

# Big issues and the experience of the Retiring Women group

This section focuses on the need for a better way of looking at retiring and the way in which people can be supported in doing just that. The three chapters offer, first, an overall analysis of themes from the stories; second, a description of the setting up of the Retiring Women group and, third, the lessons learned from running the group. The section provides a rare glimpse into an aspect of people's lives not often reported.

**Lines on Retirement, after Reading Lear**
by David Wright

*For Richard Pacholski*

*Avoid storms. And retirement parties.*
*You can't trust the sweetnesses your friends will*
*offer, when they really want your office,*
*which they'll redecorate. Beware the still*
*untested pension plan. Keep your keys. Ask*
*for more troops than you think you'll need. Listen*
*more to fools and less to colleagues. Love your*
*youngest child the most, regardless. Back to*
*storms: dress warm, take a friend, don't eat the grass,*
*don't stand near tall trees, and keep the yelling*
*down—the winds won't listen, and no one will*
*see you in the dark. It's too hard to hear*
*you over all the thunder. But you're not*
*Lear, except that we can't stop you from what*
*you've planned to do. In the end, no one leaves*
*the stage in character—we never see*
*the feather, the mirror held to our lips.*
*So don't wait for skies to crack with sun. Feel*
*the storm's sweet sting invade you to the skin,*
*the strange, sore comforts of the wind. Embrace*
*your children's ragged praise and that of friends.*
*Go ahead, take it off, take it all off.*
*Run naked into tempests. Weave flowers*
*into your hair. Bellow at cataracts.*
*If you dare, scream at the gods. Babble as*
*if you thought words could save. Drink rain like cold*
*beer. So much better than making theories.*
*We'd all come with you, laughing, if we could.*

Reprinted from *In a Fine Frenzy*,
published by the University of Iowa Press.

# Chapter 1

# Perspectives on retiring: dipping our bread into the sherry

## Caroline Lodge and Eileen Carnell

*'Retire from work, but not from life.'*

M.K. Soni

> This chapter focuses on the main themes that emerge from the stories in this book. We have pulled these together to illustrate the complex and diverse experiences of people who are in the process of retiring or who have retired. Retiring is so much more than a decision about ending paid employment. The transition involves emotional dimensions, expectations of oneself and of others, social considerations, intellectual pursuits and physical considerations as well as many other dimensions. We have not attempted an academic or theoretical account. Rather we have sought to bring together some of the key ideas that are revealed by the stories.

Many people experience the inevitability of retiring as a fearful event. One person described his experience as 'falling off a cliff'. We have met people who feel anxious about money, about what they will do with their time, how they will be seen by others and how they will see themselves, often described as concerns about identity. One of us wondered, 'who will I be in the world?' as she contemplated retiring. Others look forward to the opportunities that the change in their days will afford. The experience of retiring is much, much more than simply stopping paid work. It involves transitions in many interlinked aspects of one's life.

The complex and diverse experiences of people who are in the process of retiring or who have retired are explored in this chapter. The transitions involve emotional dimensions, expectations of oneself and of others, social considerations, intellectual pursuits and physical considerations as well as many other dimensions. We have not attempted an academic or theoretical account of retiring as we are aware of a growing literature on gerontology (that is the study of physical, mental and social changes as people age) and academic literature on transitions to retirement. Rather, this is what we would have liked to have read when we began to think seriously about retiring: real experiences to help us consider and make sense of retiring.

We begin this chapter by exploring the web of factors that influence decisions about retiring: when to go, how to go, whether to retire gradually, whether to continue with some kind of paid work in retirement and so forth.

We then move on to consider the meaning of retiring for different people and the opportunities for purposeful, valuable and satisfying activities that retirement can provide, and some factors and issues in planning for this in the transition period.

We have also noted that retiring can often mean having to face up to some uncomfortable thoughts and situations. We consider ageing, health matters, bereavement and death. We have referred to this as the dark side.

There are many ways in which people considering retiring can find support to make the best of their transition. The penultimate section explores the possibilities and advantages of these.

Finally we look at what it means to retire successfully and happily before offering some concluding comments about the experience of retiring for our generation.

## Decisions about retiring

It is not surprising that decisions about retiring can be so hard. For many of the writers in this book so much of how they understand their lives, their identities, is bound up in work. It has often provided a large portion of well-structured time, intellectual stimulation, a sense of purpose as well as social connections. The decisions reported in this book were influenced by a complex combination of factors, some related to the individuals' employment and some to other factors. First we consider some of the factors related to employment.

One factor that has emerged as highly significant in several accounts is the relationship of the individual to the organisation that they are leaving. We found many references to the organisation, which is not surprising, but we were surprised at the very strong feelings and frustrations described. Leaving paid employment is a key moment for many people to make sense of their life's work. Many surveyed their working life, searching for words that might give precision and resonance to their experiences, including their difficulties.

For some the key factor was how they had been treated by the organisation's managers. A strong confirmation of the value of their work while in employment and being treated respectfully within their organisation seems to be associated with more positive decisions. Where continuity of the work is secured the value of the work is confirmed by the organisation. Ashley wrote about the crucial discussions he was involved in about when and how to pass over responsibilities, noting that it was important to give as much notice as possible in order to help ease the transition for his colleagues. Ashley was in a good position in that he identified a new team that could be 'guardians' of his projects and that he could hand over to with confidence (Chapter 10).

Retiring seems to present people with more difficulties when they feel unvalued in their employment, when their relationship with the organisation is not or has not been good and when the continuity of the work is unsecured. In some of these stories the relationship was not very happy as members of staff make it known they are thinking of retiring. In contrast to Ashley's experience, we read of one person being given a new and unwelcome role (Eileen, Chapter 6). Diana refers to apparent indifference, adding that people's stressful, toxic work situation may contribute to people's ill-health (Chapter 12). Alison also described the higher education context as 'toxic' (Chapter 11).

However, the relationship between the person and the organisation and feelings generated are not always straightforward. Non-supportive and supportive aspects of the organisation often coexist. For example, while some experiences in organisations can be toxic, there has been much support in our organisation for people contemplating retiring, such as this publication, resources for the Retiring Women group (Chapter 2) and to run retiring workshops (Chapter 16).

The satisfaction that comes from the work is another factor in individual decisions and responses to retiring. Marianne, for example, mentions that her job was worthwhile, interesting and crucial to her identity and that it therefore seemed perverse to give it up. Her account examines how part-time work as part of a staged retirement can be an ideal solution (Chapter 7). Gil had been looking forward to developing her career when health problems forced early retirement. The adjustments were challenging (Chapter 5). Others talk about striking the right balance in making adjustments. Alex wants to continue to research and write, free from the burdens of bureaucracy (Chapter 15). Diana says she will build up a happy and self-sustaining situation in order to continue research. She points outs that as a retiree there is the huge advantage of no longer needing to earn her salary and not needing external funding to cover costs.

Ashley said he wanted to retire completely – a clean break to begin the next phase of his life. However, he goes on to say that he then 'cherry-picked' activities of particular interest. He applied for the title of emeritus professor so he could still use the library, email and a shared room, and have opportunities to respond to consultancies and research projects. This appears to be an indication of the ambivalent feelings retirees sometimes experience. They may want a 'clean break' but want to maintain strong connections at the same time.

Anne Freeman refers to a feeling of completeness and timeliness, a sense of physical readiness for retiring from teaching (Chapter 4). Her colleague Lorna refuses to apologise for her lack of regret, that she does not miss the work or the people with whom she had contact (Chapter 4). Ted felt the release from the stresses and pressures of his work when he retired on his sixty-fifth birthday (Chapter 14).

For those who retire incrementally, by reducing their hours, important negotiations need to be made so that they do not end up with too much to do and are able to cut out what is less rewarding, as Marianne testifies. Diana tells us how her institution was not good at discussing workload when she became ill, or about what would be covered while she was away, taken over by someone else or be dropped permanently. She suggested early retirement on the grounds of ill-health and to be brought back for one-third time for two years to ease herself back into her new situation. However, adjusting felt uncomfortable and, like others we have spoken to, she missed the demands of a busy, full-time role. Marianne highlights the potential problem of feeling excluded and overlooked, although she points out that part-timers may be included in many different, important aspects of work and be offered the same opportunities as full-time workers. Later she felt the reduction from three days a week was a much less traumatic change than the initial decision to scale down.

Difficulties of being in a different relationship with the organisation can continue through the transition. Space and place appears to be very important when colleagues are in the process of retiring and in transition – a gradual separation from the physical organisation. Some colleagues who still have some connection with their organisation but no dedicated place to work in it experience transitional difficulties. Eileen became aware that she had no opportunity to control her workspace and felt displaced when 'hot-desking' was required. Diana has always done most of her 'real work' at home and acknowledges that she did not experience this problem.

Decisions about retirement are also influenced in these accounts by factors other than employment and the organisation for which one works. Negotiations, often lengthy, are needed with the place of work and colleagues, but also with partner, family or others. For some these negotiations were easy, with the relevant others being totally supportive. Others experienced a period of turbulence. What emerges is that people need to build in time to discuss what is happening in their lives and how differences and potential difficulties can be acknowledged and attended to. Marianne's partner had already retired and she says: 'We were out of step with each other'.

The transition nearly always means a reconsideration of priorities, as noted in Barbara's account (Chapter 4). For some the desire to pursue other interests becomes compelling, as reported by Jennifer, Alex and many others. Some commitments may make readjustments necessary, for example where care of others is involved. We know of colleagues whose decision to retire was compelled by the need to care for aged relatives. Others have chosen to care for their grandchildren. Some wish to lessen the physical demands of their lives, or had that forced upon them. Some people choose to continue to make a contribution but in a different way, especially through volunteering or consultancy work.

The many different ways in which the writers made their decision to retire are fascinatingly varied. Making the decision 'in a flash' is how Marianne describes it – a moment in her car when it became obvious what she needed to do. She felt liberated and felt a split second of excitement rather than despondency or even fear at the thought of retirement. Then followed a series of interlinked decisions – a move from full- to part-time work, setting a date for formal retirement and then a decision to work more flexibly after that.

In a completely different way, Caroline (Chapter 13) imagined herself five years in the future and worked backwards from that ideal place, calculating and planning what she needed to do each year in order to get to that point. (A description of this activity can be found in Chapter 16.) This helped her after a period of indecision and not knowing how to prepare, having no criteria on which to make a decision. Some, quite simply, came to the decision when their age suggested it, when the opportunity to claim their pensions made the decisions straightforward, usually at 60 for women and 65 for men. Barbara decided to retire at 61 to give her time to start a new life before getting too old to want to move or change. Anne Freeman felt that running a large department was too demanding physically and emotionally and that she lacked stamina to do the job effectively. Lorna said she was ready for the next phase; it was time to move on and for that she was not sorry. There were some disappointments and frustrations around decisions to retire. For example, Eileen's hope to retire early led to a disappointment when the organisation turned down an application, and Diana's intention to step into retirement with minimal changes to her life was dashed when she was diagnosed with cancer.

Ashley says that the decision to retire crept up on him and then he began to think about it increasingly. In Ashley's case the experience of three close family members was pivotal in his decision. Most significant was the totally unexpected and shocking death of his wife (aged 53) and of his father-in-law within a year of retiring. However, his own father retired at 50 and then had 40 years living a varied and fulfilled life. Ashley aspires to be like his father.

He reflects on his own 40-year career and on the powerful feelings about ending a fortunate, successful and happy working life in which he had reached positions he had never dreamt of. However, his enthusiasm for work was beginning to wane and he began to have new and different aspirations.

We also note that the occasion to mark leaving paid work can be significant, partly because it can be a public affirmation of a person's value to colleagues. Ashley wanted his leaving party to be a positive occasion as it was a once-in-a-lifetime event – not a formal affair, with all staff invited and held at a convenient time and place. He planned every detail with colleagues. The highly successful event was the result of careful planning and he left with a 'warm feeling'. Others refer to the importance of marking the occasion in the most appropriate way, reflecting the retiree's personal preference. For example, Marianne felt it was important to acknowledge and celebrate her achievements and what a good job she had made of combining her career and family life. One thing that emerged is that each person needs to be consulted about their 'event' and be included in its planning. Diana said she would not feel comfortable at the centre of a celebratory party and for her a day to celebrate some aspects of her work was more appropriate. Gil recalls how her sudden departure meant she had no time to complete anything. 'I never returned, apart from a visit to say goodbye at the end-of-term meeting and a later visit to clear my desk.' A choice to leave with no event at all needs to be respected even though many of us think that the end of a career warrants special attention. Not all retiring parties are happy events, as David Wright suggests in his poem *Lines on Retirement, after Reading Lear* (see page 2), which begins, 'Avoid storms. And retirement parties.'

This group of retirees may be unusual in that most of them had a degree of choice. For some people it is a matter of reaching a fixed age that forces them to retire even when they don't want to, or some have to work longer than they would like as they have a much lower income. In this book, we read that a large number of people chose to retire gradually, either by going part-time or taking on consultancy work, very often out of interest and love of the work they do and/or thinking that a phased period would help them during the transition, and wanting to continue to make a contribution.

### The meaning and opportunities of retiring

We delight in the writers' metaphors and images of retiring. Some are amusing, some strike a chord and some are brutal. These metaphors deserve attention as they reveal new understandings about transitions and retiring. We were struck by Alex's 'into the airlock' metaphor conjuring up transitional space – the space entered by the astronaut. The metaphor works in two ways depending on whether he sees himself as the astronaut or the ship. Either way the airlock constitutes a rather scary, solitary space in which he is cocooned, slightly detached, but which offers security – a temporary halfway house offering the possibility of return. For Alex this is an appealing approach to retirement. At the moment: 'retirement seems a bit of a void, welcoming in its endless possibilities, but simultaneously frightening in its emptiness and lack of recognisable reference points'. As his perspective changes the metaphor won't be necessary. He will have completed the transition and settled into the life he has chosen. Barbara conjures up a similar image in a dream. She is also in a spaceship. When the door opens she will be sucked into oblivion. She waits calmly. Barbara thinks this represents how she copes with endings, cutting off feelings and not facing up to losses.

Other metaphors raise a smile of recognition, for example the journey to which Sid refers, crossing the threshold and arriving at the other side (Chapter 17).

The idea of retiring can carry negative connotations, especially about how one is seen or sees oneself (Maguire 2008). These ideas are often described as related to a sense of identity. For example, Marianne says that moving into life as an 'old person' is hard to accept. She refers to a research report that suggests a small minority of people wake up on their first day of retirement feeling sad, anxious or lost (DWP 2008).

Other fears can be about loss of structure or purpose to the day, loss of social connections, or the sense of being useful or purposeful. Marianne has accepted that she is not going to progress in her career and will lose status. Anne Gold talks about having to come to terms with a lower profile and loss of respect. Her work structure supports her construct of herself and she is now at the stage of redefining what it is to be useful (Chapter 9). Barbara wonders whether without the structure of her job she may feel lost. She also worries about purpose, identity and usefulness. Alex is ambivalent. He says he can see retiring as either a 'happy haven' or, on a gloomier side, 'an indication that old age has arrived, the best of life is past, days depressingly and uncontrovertibly numbered and the chance and time to achieve gone'.

Retiring is often seen as a series of transitions from one way of being to another – from work to retiring. Marianne says, 'the concept of being in transition is valid. Moving into retirement is not going to be the last transition'. Barbara said she was lucky to have had transitions in school in the previous five years during which she downsized from a very responsible position. Leaving became easier. Diana suggests she is beginning to accept that she is no longer, and never will be again, 'doing the same thing as before but without the bits I don't like. I am somewhere different'. This sense of being in transit is complex, and can be seen as problematic or liberating, or both at the same time.

Leaving employment usually has implications for how time is spent. While many people look forward to a more restful time others embrace new occupations. In the Retiring Women group we often refer to a recipe for a good day: some exercise, a good laugh and achieving something. Anne Freeman is surprised she is enjoying herself so much: 'relishing the feeling'. She has begun ambitious projects in photography which allows her to share her gardening achievements with her daughter who lives in Vancouver. Her colleague Lorna is joyful and says that at last there is the time to do the things she dreamed about – writing the novel alongside lots of other projects and doing stuff 'for the hell of it'.

Dare to dream, advises Jacqui in Chapter 16. The fantasies that sustained the contributors throughout their working lives may now become realities, like Alex's and Lorna's novels, or Gil's dream to make large ceramic pots. However, stepping into the dream life may not be as easy as they imagined. Alison is fulfilling a long-held ambition to have an authentic French experience. This was not an easy journey and she had a 'frightening and lonely' first year. She is alarmed by the ease in which she can mix only with other English people and speak English all the time. But she needs their knowledge and support, so this is a dilemma for her. Alex senses a loss of a fantasy. He could tell himself that work was temporary but now he has to get on with it.

At first retirees may experience a new sense of freedom. Jennifer explains: 'I am like a kid in a sweetshop, waking up each morning thinking of all the delightful range of activities, what will I choose today?' She appreciates the chance to follow the natural rhythms of her body – to rest, sleep or be active when she needs to. Much of the 'extra' time is saved from being freed from long commutes to and from work (Chapter 8). Diana concurs, saying it is wonderful to be able to take it easy when feeling unwell, to see more of grandchildren and friends, and to plan exciting trips. Jennifer describes a new phase of life which links more closely to her personal and emotional history as well as directing her to a different future. Gil now delights in the adventures and possibilities open to her, and in the changes of the previous ten years.

A number of writers speak about how the quality of their lives is changing – not having to get up before sunrise and not having to be crammed into a tube carriage in the rush hour every day. Lorna remarks: 'I can enjoy the whole of the weekend … the black cloud won't descend mid-Sunday afternoon.'

Across the accounts we read about 'busy' days. Indeed, two writers refer to this in their chapter titles. After work life gets busier, for some. But the activities described are not frivolous, far from it. Changing priorities means it is now easier to do what the Retiring Women group have called feeding the soul. This means different things to different people, but can involve travel, poetry, art, painting, ballet, singing, other creative activities, reading, walking, laughing, crying, talking, togetherness. Jennifer values most highly the skills that 'bring us closer to most of humanity – growing and preparing food, looking after children, nurturing our families and living well in our communities'.

A similar message comes across in Anne Freeman's account in experimenting with new dishes as well as being involved in nature conservation. We note the underpinning desire to do things well, be involved in worthy causes and not waste time.

The accounts are bursting with descriptions of the way they are using, redefining, transferring, developing and learning new skills, including: grand-parenting, new languages including French, Spanish, Chinese, enrolling on courses (some accredited), art, music and singing, volunteering, writing, keeping fit and healthy, refurbishing homes, playing squash, golf, walking and travelling, doing crosswords to help ward off Alzheimer's, relaxing, writing poetry and novels, photography and, as Alex puts it, to find out more about the wondrous workings of the universe. Ashley points out that unintended, unplanned activities are welcome including for him: joining a fitness centre, theatre, concert and cinema visits, French classes, making contact with longstanding friends, poetry, play readings and travel.

Jennifer expands on the importance of grand-parenting and in helping her grandchildren learn in a safe space. As well as the fun and good feeling of not being ultimately responsible she is able to help them learn about cooking and preparing healthy food, seasonality and what food looks like when it is growing. Her time grand-parenting allows her own children to follow their careers. She points out that this type of activity where people feel involved and useful are two important antidotes to getting old and depressed. Anne Gold also talks about the joy of doing things she previously never had time for which she thought were less important than work. She says that as a mother she was never relaxed having young babies around because she also had her work, house and home. Now she gets tremendous joy out of just watching her grandchildren develop communication.

The myth that retiring life is a permanent holiday was shattered. Alison points out that there are always things to do in the house and garden. She and Jennifer highlight the need for real holidays and trips away from home to get away from all responsibilities no matter how much they have been diminished by giving up work. Some contributors are planning slightly different holidays that reduce aeroplane travel and consequently their carbon footprint.

There are opinions too about what we don't have to do any more. Marianne sent us the following email message:

*I had another thought about the benefits of being older (retiring). It suddenly struck me that there was real relief involved with 'all the things I don't have to do any more'. This will be different for everyone, but for me it includes a lot of sports-type things that I always felt I ought to try or try to improve, but did not really want to. Now in my sixties I really don't have to play tennis (badly) anymore or ever try snorkeling and can look back with satisfaction on the fact that I did once try to ski and did once drive a quad bike, but that at my advanced age don't have to do either of those things again!*

Some people want to use their wisdom and experience in political ways and to contribute to society. Scale is not seen as important. Ashley is considering working with older people as a volunteer. Being a school grandparent governor is one way of fulfilling an important role and keeping in touch with educational issues for Jennifer. Diana is also a school governor and a government advisory committee member. Eileen works as a Samaritan volunteer. Jennifer feels that having an allotment is a subversive activity, resisting the control of life by big organisations. She likes the idea of being subversive and dangerous. Alison is becoming involved in local politics in her new community in France. Diana anticipates becoming political and community-focused again and hopes to return to more political and cutting-edge writing.

Some writers highlight unexpected events and identify the need to plan for an integration of new patterns of living. They talk about the need to plan their days, some experiment and find that over-planning creates too much structure. For example, Eileen is trying to overcome her tendency to have a timetable for every day, although Alison points out that some degree of structure provides a safety net. Marianne feels a diary entry works like magic, telling her what she was supposed to do and thus avoiding the trap of working on the days she is not being paid for. Anne Freeman concurs. She found that when she reduced her timetable to 0.8 fte she spent her day off doing school work. Alex is learning to cope without the given structures and routines of work. He likens this to a rescued animal being released into the wild, 'a tad scary, a world without structure, security and predictability'. But he has learned that he can now enjoy what each day brings.

Anne Gold points out that for women the transition to retirement may be easier if they are able to continue the responsibilities they have always had outside work. She says that, as a woman, working life was never just about work: 'There were all sorts of other strands and responsibilities going on. … Women have many focuses, men don't. I often felt torn about all the things I had to do but now it's less hurried.'

Many people rely on work for much of their social life. Diana suggests people need substitutes for the status, community and companionship they had in the workplace. Caroline talks about her work community as important in social terms, being productive and receiving respect. This helped her understand her reluctance in taking steps to retire as she had to consider how to replace the social connections provided by work.

Being retired may provide the opportunities to create new social relationships, especially through shared activities such as visits to galleries, films, walking, walking holidays and shopping with friends. Some writers have described how they deliberately set up new communities or networks in anticipation. Others describe how being at home, often alone, may mean more deliberate attention to seeing people on a regular basis. For example, in her first year abroad, Alison started a number of groups that meet regularly, for friendship, sewing, reading and walking.

In two accounts retirees have talked about the importance of having a new dog in their lives. The benefits of having a dog are that they provide a clear structure to the day, ensure regular exercise, provide security and companionship.

An individual's retiring can affect a number of people. Alison talks about how some of her friends in England were unhappy with her choice to live abroad. Readjustments are required on all sides. Assumptions may arise about the availability of the person who is seen to have 'spare' time – the one to go to the dry cleaners! Expectations of partners can be intensified. When one partner is free to develop new interests and to travel it can create tensions. Eileen reports how occasionally her partner felt excluded. We want to highlight the differences in family groupings and lifestyle and what this means for retirees. Different tensions can emerge in any of these situations: having children, not having children, having grandchildren, being partnered, being single.

It is likely that retiring includes making decisions about one's home: the size and location of the living space. Where you live, who you live with and how you connect with communities can be important decisions, and some may consider moving to more communal accommodation such as co-housing, or to a smaller place. Barbara found herself needing to reassess her priorities. She has co-owned her house for the last 16 years and it now has to be sold. She said that sorting out the house was more of a roller coaster than any feelings about retiring. Eileen came to realise the importance of one's relationship with space and in her home took time to decorate and make it more pleasant for entertaining and being sociable. She has made a symbolic gesture of converting her study into a studio.

Keeping in good health is a high priority. We read how contributors are getting together to engage in activities that are physical as well as social. Swimming, Jennifer claims, is the ideal exercise for those between 60 and 70. Alison is a keen skier and Caroline, Barbara and Eileen enthusiastic practitioners of Pilates. Some people say they are getting tired and are coming to terms with physical changes.

Two other aspects of life are often mentioned and one not. Depression is voiced a lot. In our Retiring Women group we question its function and wonder why it is common among retiring people and if this is about putting off difficult decisions or a chosen state to numb painful transitions. Financial implications are mentioned a lot too. There is concern that pensions will not be adequate. However, Marianne points out that when it is possible to top up one's income with consultancy, combined with the reduction of the day-to-day expenses of going to work, this can soften the impact of the loss of earnings. Some recurring financial themes are discussed in Chapter 17. In contrast, the sexual aspects of life are not often discussed. These are private, but in talking with each other and in the group we have come to see that these remain important aspects of life and need attention.

## The darker side of retiring

We have struggled with this aspect, identifying the connection between retiring, physical decline and ageing. We find ourselves challenged in our view of ourselves. We may resent the lack of esteem for older people, and the invisibility that we experience. And we have to face bereavement by the death of those we love, and our own mortality.

Identities can be challenging when retiring and/or at times of change or transitions, irrespective of gender, though specifics for reframing and rebuilding identities and self-esteem are often gender-specific. These are discussed at length by Anne Gold.

Alex says he went through an uncomfortable process of assessing and reassessing life, the need to put failure into a tolerable perspective and be more positive about achievements. He wonders if he will experience a loss of identity and a feeling of no longer contributing to society. Gil provides a vivid account of being faced with severe disability from her fifties. Although she recovered her mobility, Gil has had to face up to an incomplete career, and the experience of unfulfilled potential.

Some write about how they see themselves as a retiree and getting older. New images are created, new clothes bought, news ways of behaviour demonstrated. Discussion focuses on how do you live to convey the person you want to be. A definition that Eileen borrowed, 'a process of reconstructing and navigating new identities' (Ecclestone *et al.* 2005), seems to convey this complex task.

During our third, annual residential weekend of the Retiring Women group some controversial discussion occurred around our changing views on our presence in the world as older people. There was ambivalence and some tensions for us, especially about changing identities. One of us spoke about being able to sense a time line and able to plot how we see ourselves in the world over time and how others see us. For example, we spoke about our ambivalent feelings when people offer to stand for us on the bus. While we sometimes appreciate the sign of respect we wonder whether those offering their seats consider us as frailer. And depending on our mood we either accept graciously or refuse elegantly protesting that we are perfectly fit. Some of us are proud of the bright orange plastic covers of our travel Freedom Pass; others hide them in discreet wallets.

Our advancing age also raises issues of visibility and invisibility. Some of us feel excluded when young people seem not to notice us. Marianne pointed out in an email that:

*One of the major benefits of being older is not suffering the excruciating self-consciousness of youth. I know we don't like being invisible to the young on pavements and train platforms, but there is a wonderful freedom in it too. Doris Lessing describes this in* The Summer Before the Dark (see Appendix).

It may not come across explicitly in the narratives but ageism has been a frequent topic in our discussions. The ageist society in which we live is particularly unkind to women. Issues of ageism affect men and women differently, as Anne reflects in Chapter 9. We have talked about the feelings aroused about being 'invisible' and the negative manner in which women are portrayed in the media. One of us is conducting a project to photograph older women while retiring, intending to challenge their invisibility. One of the books we recommend, *50 over 50* (see Appendix), was sponsored by the company Dove that aims to portray older women in a positive way. New products constantly advertised by the anti-ageism cosmetic industry astonish us and we despair at how cosmetic surgery is discussed as fairly normal in some media. One advertisement for face cream says this may be a good product, 'if you are not ready for cosmetic procedures'. As if we will ever be! For men this issue seems confined to hair treatments and virility products.

From the members of our group who travel overseas for conferences, research and teaching we hear how other cultures, especially in some parts of Asia, Africa and India perceive women differently as they grow older. They gain more respect in some cultures and their wisdom and maturity are recognised as important. We wonder about the necessity of giving the age of a woman for a media story whatever her position or role in society and how women actors are said to look great – 'for their age'.

We are moved by the writers' memories and insights on the issue of death and bereavement. In their stories the participants are often open about the pain of particular losses and the challenges of the deaths of close family and friends. Bereavement is a common experience. Many of us have lost one or both parents. Jennifer expresses a recent bereavement in a very moving way. She would have liked more time with her mother to talk and look after her. She misses her profoundly and the things that she does now in this period of retiring, such as gardening and making jam, are 'a sort of homage to her and her way of life which was so different to my own'. Caroline misses her close friend Archie who died sadly within a year of his retirement. Situations are discussed where bereavement led to depression for several years.

Bereavement is a particularly relevant issue for people who are retiring as often deaths occur when difficult life-adjusting decisions are being made. So people who are retiring may also be going through the complicated process of grieving which may encompass many different emotional responses. Some people may face many years without a partner or close friend and their retiring years are lonely.

We are all facing death and for some retiring appears to be the last stage before it comes. We are aware that in our culture death is a taboo subject and we do not mention our own death in our writing or discussions. Some are preparing, revising wills, putting papers in order and making wishes known about funerals. The *Natural Death Handbook* has helpful guidance about leaving one's affairs in an orderly fashion (see Appendix). Other titles in our bibliography in the Appendix have been found to be particularly helpful to those of us who have been trying to understand death and the process of bereavement and those of us who have been able to consider our own.

## Support for retiring

Sharing concerns and finding very specific help is noted in the narratives. It is striking how often writers refer to the value of conversations with others about retiring. The members of the Retiring Women group appreciate the help in seeing oneself differently and in making sense of a new kind of life. Anne Gold says the group helped by providing a space dedicated to thinking about retiring issues and to hearing other people's plans. She says, 'I think if I hadn't thought about retirement, if I hadn't reflected on it and tried to make sense of it before, it would have hit me quite painfully'. She added that she still needed a woman-only space to help deal better with gendered life. Caroline mentioned specific support, 'to provide inspiration for creativity and ideas for activities to enhance the quality of life'. She values the regular meetings to check on her well-being, deliberations and plans. Some felt the group was helpful but could have been more challenging: Diana said that she suspected that being a professor gave her licence 'to spout on' as if she knew what she was doing, rather than helping her be clearer about her boundaries and priorities.

Caroline attended a pre-retirement course and while she did not fit in with that group of people found it helpful in seeing that planning was a good thing. She also had a retirement consultant and this resulted in reducing the number of days she worked but didn't really help her make longer-term decisions. Ashley also attended a pre-retirement course and highlights the benefits in his account.

Diana thought that some mentoring would have been helpful at one stage when she was unable to be systematic about changing her practices or how she thought about herself. She mentioned that later in the retiring process a personal coach 'might have buoyed me up, made me see that things would not go on as before and kept me on track'. Others looking to the future thought that getting advice from people who work freelance or getting a life coach would be helpful (Chapter 16).

It is noted that it takes a great deal of time to attend to financial issues. Seeking help from a financial adviser is important. Ashley saw three and was then happy in the way he invested his money. He, like others, decided to take the biggest lump sum. The majority of the contributors are in a strong position financially and are aware that this eases the retiring process.

Many of the contributors have identified, either in their stories or to us in correspondence, that the process of preparing and writing their account, their self-searching, has been of positive benefit. Alex says it proved a curiously therapeutic exercise and helped him get through a difficult transition more quickly than if he had been left to his own devices. The pressure he was putting on himself to achieve or the pressure of self-accusation at not having achieved has gone. Now he is more productive than ever.

People also found it helpful to keep a reflective diary (Barbara's account focuses on how she made sense of her feelings in a difficult time of transitions through a reflective analysis), seek out the professional support of a dietician and engage a personal fitness tutor.

In the narratives some literature was cited as being particularly helpful for contributors (see references at the end of each chapter) and we have included an appendix with an annotated bibliography.

## Thinking about what retiring successfully might mean

Contributors have indicated a wish not to present a stereotypical image of retirees, especially in being active. Retiring successfully and/or ageing actively are much-contested concepts in the academic field of gerontology. Some of our writers have suggested that some accounts need to come with a warning. Very active lifestyles do not suit everybody. Some people cannot or do not want to be active and choosing more sedentary occupations should not be seen as any less important or beneficial. Writers feel that we should not brush off the downsides of retiring and of getting older. One email question from Marianne asked, 'is there enough about the dark side?' Diana points out that getting older and illness can upset everything at any time: 'Being seriously ill, and getting through chemotherapy, is itself a full-time job'. Ashley, too, warns that physical injuries may take longer to heal as one gets older.

In email discussions about the book there was also some concern expressed about our not coming across as being too prissy. Perhaps meeting for cocktails, cinema outings to *Mama Mia* and other less sober occasions need to be noted. Perhaps frivolity is not something that scholars and educationalists think fitting for their narratives and so they have left out of their accounts references to the fun they are having. And if any of us live to a ripe old age they may want to express a similar sentiment to that of Edna McLure. Edna celebrated her 109th birthday in Blackley, Manchester, by revealing that the secret of her long life was eating bread dipped in sherry (*The Observer*, 31 August 2008: 8). We like this image and have borrowed it for the title of this chapter.

There are moments when the contributors talk about feelings of joy, feeling more alive, more powerful and healthier and many find retiring a very positive experience. An optimistic future is presented in a survey in *The Independent* (4 April 2002). It reported that Britons are happiest between the ages of 65 and 74 (survey for the pharmacists, Boots). It reported that people experience a rise in well-being during life, which peaks after retirement. The Policy Studies Institute asked 48 men and women how they'd coped with retirement. It found the happiest were those in couples, who had strong ideas about what they wanted to do and saw retirement as an opportunity to see friends and develop interests. It also found that having enough money and being in good health increased the chances of a happy retirement (*The Guardian* Weekend Magazine, 20 September 2008).

## Some concluding thoughts

This book was written in 2008/9. This has particular significance for a number of reasons. We who are retiring at this time are particularly fortunate and we want to point out that retiring now is very different from previous generations and will be for those to come. For example, Anne Gold observes that gender issues may be different in the future.

As we write this chapter research results from the Office for National Statistics indicate that there are now more pensioners in Britain than under-sixteens with explosive consequences for the NHS and pensions (*The Independent*, 22 August 2008: 1). The over-eighties represent the fastest growing section of the population. This has implications for spending on the health service, investment in better care homes, issues around dignity in dying, preventing ageist insurance, travel companies' policies, promoting more positive images of the elderly and for flexible working arrangements (Margaret Drabble, *The Observer*, 24 August 2008: 31) and massive investment in research into dementia (Mervyn Kohler, Special Adviser for Help the Aged).

Diana can see useful ways for a senior academic to continue to contribute professional expertise, prior to and beyond retirement. She had a sense of marginalisation that did not encourage the best from her while she was employed or since. More generally, it does not support what could be potentially a wonderful, large post-retirement voluntary workforce – which could bring the university prestige, support fundraising and develop its involvement in the local community. Diana cited research evidence in a survey of retired academics and academic-related staff that universities did not recognise the actual or potential contribution of retired academics (Tizard and Owen 2001: 268).

Lorna brings to our attention that we are part of the baby boom generation, 'apparently we'd never had it so good'. She continues, 'we were the new generation, forging ahead, carving out new paths, new ways of thinking and juggling career with looking after baby'. One of the positive aspects of the baby boom generation, on the whole, is that retirees are more confident, self- conscious and relatively wealthy. The baby boom generation has more disposable income in their sixties than their predecessors, leading to the concept of the 'grey pound'. In large numbers this group is more able to make demands and have their voices heard. For example, they are more likely to vote than the younger generation so politicians are more aware of them and their demands. These 60 year olds don't take being sidelined easily and wield increasing political clout. They are more widely travelled than previous generations and they have seen huge developments in their lifetime, for example, in television, film and the Internet. There is now a raised awareness of health and many opportunities to prolong a fit and healthy lifestyle. There are more entitlements too, to support a healthier older age (Chapter 18, Reasons to be cheerful). Lorna rejoices: 'I'm free and I've got the Freedom Pass to prove it. ... The best thing that ever happened to pensioners'. It should also be noted that we are mainly Londoners and have advantages not available to others who live elsewhere.

There are difficult aspects, however. There is a so-called 'sandwich generation' in which people in their fifties or early sixties may have both children in their twenties or thirties and elderly parents who are living longer to support. Their children may have student loans, can't afford their own property or are unable to get a mortgage. At the same time their elderly parents may need to be supported either financially, emotionally or in very practical ways. So members of this sandwich generation may have to work part- or full-time in order to support their children and parents. In 1908 the Pension Act came into force and as we write we celebrate its hundredth birthday. But the state pension age for all will rise to 68 by 2046.

The people who have shared their stories have had very interesting and fulfilling careers and are searching to make their new lives interesting and fulfilling too. Helpful observations are made about transitions, ups and downs, of adjusting to new ways of being and newly forming identities. Some look for satisfaction from paid work, others through volunteering, caring for others or by taking up challenging new pursuits. They all talk about trying to live fit and healthy lives and some are experiencing the challenge of living with illness.

They are remarkable and strong people and it has been a privilege to read and comment on their narratives. We have been moved, amused, surprised and delighted by their individual accounts, as we intend our readers to be.

We have learned much from the collective picture and have developed a new understanding of the retiring process.

## References

Department of Work and Pensions (DWP) (2008) *Research published on how retirement feels,* 8 April, London, Departmental Press Release.

Ecclestone, K., Blackmore, T., Biesta, G., Colley, H. and Hughes, M. (2005) 'Transitions through the lifecourse: political, professional and academic perspectives'. Paper presented at the Annual TLRP/ESRC Conference, University of Warwick.

Maguire, M. (2008) 'End of term: teacher identities in a post-work context'. *Pedagogy, Culture and Society,* 16(1), March, 43–55.

Tizard, B. and Owen, C. (2001) 'Activities and attitudes of retired university staff'. *Oxford Review of Education,* 27(2), 253–70.

# The history of the Retiring Women group

## Marianne Coleman

*'Life begins at retirement.'*

Anon.

This chapter describes the history and setting up of the Retiring Women group. It includes a description of the way the group started, its first and subsequent residential experience, and the way in which meetings were organised and run. It outlines the support given to its members and touches on the achievements of the group, including the writing of this book. Many of these themes are picked up and developed in other chapters in the book, especially in Chapter 3 where we discuss what we have learned from running the group.

In the summer of 2005 a group of eight of us were fortunate to be asked by a colleague, Alison Kirton, lecturer at the Institute of Education, if we would like to meet up to talk about issues around retiring. Our average age was then approaching 60. We did not all know each other well, but there were lots of friendship and/or work links within the group. The first meeting was totally informal and involved sitting in a nearby London square eating and drinking, talking and laughing. We all enjoyed it and decided to arrange another meeting. Since then we have met for two hours at least once a month, and have got to know each other better. Through our discussions we have drawn strength from the group to face up to the challenges of retiring. As well as meeting regularly we also spent a residential weekend together in February 2006, April 2007 and May 2008. There have also been purely social spin-offs from the group. There is a circle that extends well beyond the group that meets frequently to eat at vegetarian restaurants. There have also been shopping trips, walks, lunches, cocktails and a stitching group that involve others outside the group.

There are no formal rules for the group, but we do take it in turns to arrange a venue for a meeting and provide some refreshments. If a member of the group cannot attend a meeting one of us makes sure that the things discussed are passed on. Normally each meeting starts with general conversation and then we go round the group so that each member has a chance to talk and receive feedback from the others.

A lot of the things that continue to be discussed within the group have arisen from the first weekend we spent together from a Friday afternoon to a Monday afternoon in February 2006. We had an external facilitator, and worked through sessions that we planned together in two meetings before the weekend. We started with looking in pairs at a visual representation of our life-line and ended by individually writing down three things that we decided to do. In between we looked at the issues that concerned us. Some of the things we agreed before the weekend were that:

- The outcomes would be unique to each person
- We might challenge each other but we would be respectful in doing so
- We would give honest reactions and commit to work with the reactions
- We would acknowledge differences.

In the evaluation of the weekend the group members identified several important ways in which this event strengthened them as individuals and as a group.

In the first year we spent a lot of time discussing what being a full-time member of an organisation meant and what issues there were for us in 'letting go'. It was good to have a safe place where we could discuss the different feelings that emerged in working in a particular organisation. We were able to support each other in ensuring that the 'ending' or 'endings' were as appropriate and healthy as possible. As members of the group started leaving the organisation other issues emerged, as can be seen from the stories that follow.

By April 2007 three of the group had retired and we had all moved a little further in our understandings of the sorts of transitions we were going through. The discussions were meaningful and wide ranging as before, but also included more consideration of the practicalities involved with retiring and ageing. We thought about health issues and our goals, aims and plans, taking into account physical, emotional and intellectual needs and the desire to be useful. By the time of our most recent weekend away in May 2008, the majority of us had retired and we had been meeting regularly for nearly three years. Most of our meeting time on this occasion was spent by each person reviewing the last year, and, with feedback from the group, planning for the future and setting goals to be reviewed at future meetings.

All groups go through stages of development, summed up by Tuckman (1985) as 'forming, storming, norming and performing'. Inevitably there are tensions involved and some of those that the group have faced include:

- The tensions between meeting to provide a social network, providing support to others and 'working' on issues.
- What happens when people do not come into the organisation as they do not work there any more and find that the long journey means that they do not attend meetings as regularly, and other commitments and priorities may be more pressing.
- The tensions between different statuses/relationships people have both in the organisation and outside, for example in work being more 'senior' in the organisation's hierarchy or working in the organisation for a longer or shorter time.
- Outside work, differences like being married or not married, living with a partner or living alone, having heterosexual or lesbian relationships make a big difference to the issues faced by individual retiring women.

We all have our own particular needs from membership of the group. Preparing for a new phase of life is never easy and retiring from work means changes in the way you spend many of your waking hours. There are the positives: time to spend sorting out all the things you have put off; travelling; developing a hobby or finding one. There is the downside of a probable loss in perceived status and there are challenges in renegotiating lifestyle with your partner and/or significant others. People nearing or at retirement age may be facing a reduction in energy levels and physical ailments varying from minor aches and pains to life-threatening conditions. At the very least they will be aware of the need to keep or improve their levels of fitness. For the generation who have now reached or are approaching 60 there is the particularly irritating realisation that, contrary to all expectations, we are actually getting old.

We have not so far arranged for 'experts' to discuss finance, health or other practical issues with us, but we would certainly do that if we felt as a group that it was what we wanted. We have found it useful to exchange practical information between us about the sorts of interests and activities that we might want to develop during this time of our lives.

Our most recent development is the writing of this book. There is very little written about retirement other than practical hints on how to manage the finances (Chapter 17 focuses on this area and useful references are given in the Appendix). We found nothing that 'spoke' directly to us in our progress towards and into retirement. We hope that the personal reflections included here will be helpful to others thinking about this important stage in their lives whether singly or in a group like ours.

## Reference

Tuckman, B.W. (1985) 'Developmental sequence in small groups'. *Psychological Bulletin*, 63.

Chapter 3

# What we have learned about running the group

Eileen Carnell, Marianne Coleman,
Jennifer Evans, Anne Gold, Alison Kirton,
Diana Leonard, Caroline Lodge, Anne Peters

*'We grow neither better or worse as we grow old, but more like ourselves.'*

May Lamberton Becker

> This chapter is intended to assist others who may be thinking of running a group to support them in thinking about retiring. It includes significant decisions we took when the group was established, as well as issues and challenges that have arisen as we have continued to develop as a group.

This chapter records the reflections of the members of the Retiring Women group about the running of the group. While this cannot be completely separated from the purposes and content of the group sessions, reported in Chapter 2, we feel that it is worth writing a separate chapter on the processes of the group. In this chapter we consider:

- the group's ways of working
- challenges, working with differences
- changes in the group over time
- facilitation
- mundane considerations (food, meeting place, timings, communications between times)

- what we have done as a result, and
- what we've learned about being a group.

The review we conducted to inform this chapter confirmed for us that periodic reviews are very helpful, even if they are not wholly comfortable. The chapter has two sections: starting up, and ongoing processes and challenges.

### Starting up

Three features of the group were important in starting up: the commonalities, the particular members and expectations of membership.

### Commonalities

The eight women in our group have in common age, gender, experience of working in the same institution (although in different roles), and being in transition, as well as values and sensitivities to working in groups. Our focus was on retiring. A mixed group could have run in the same way as our all-women group. We are not suggesting that other groups need to have the same set of things in common as ours, but we do suggest that when a group comes together members are explicit about any commonalities and differences, and about their significance for the purposes of the group.

### Membership

There were several important decisions for the group related to membership. The first decision was the way in which the group is put together. Our group was initiated by one person (Alison), who chose women she knew would get on together. There was then some snowballing (i.e. one person recommended another). Members of other groups may have little knowledge of each other.

The decision to be a closed group was made after the third session. We had to make an early decision, to which we have stuck despite considerable interest by others (mainly women, but some men) who have understood the value of the group to our members and want to join us. We remain a group of eight, which is a good size for a group. So the next decisions were the size of the group and whether to accept new members.

Following that we decided about the frequency and duration of the meetings. Our group meets once a month for about two hours. Not all groups would decide on this frequency or length of meeting. We have also arranged three residential weekends (at intervals of about 13 months). We did not plan to do this at the outset. We may not choose to have another one. It will be a group decision.

We don't know what the group will do when people leave. This has not yet been an issue we have had to confront, but we are aware that three years has been a long time in the life of the group. We have expressed great value in the support from the group, and know how important such a community can be, especially in times of transitions.

It is a feature of a group of people who are retiring, and at different stages, that their lives will take them in different places. One of our members lives in France, others have daytime commitments (including work) or live too far to make a journey to central London an easy option. Frequently one or more members are committed overseas, or in another part of the country at the time of our monthly meetings. Consequently we rarely have all eight members together, and sometimes there are as few as four. Recognising that members will be able to make different commitments to the group and that these might change over time has been important from the outset and remains a challenge.

## Group processes and challenges

### Ground rules

We set up some ground rules early on, and these are reviewed more or less explicitly from time to time. Our ground rules or contract are closely linked to our purposes and are underpinned therefore by our understandings of how trust develops, the importance of active listening and respect, respecting differences in experiences, relationships, emotional states, confidentiality, tolerance and humour.

For us it was important that we had a rule of *confidentiality* – what is said in the group stays within the group. This is especially important because we all work or have worked in the same institution. But confidentiality is important for any group looking at transitions in members' lives, as it creates the climate for confidence and for challenge. It allows us to explore the dark side of retiring alongside the challenges and opportunities.

We have built up trust between the members, largely by being receptive and responsive to the needs and situations of each other. A significant part of this is acknowledging differences in experiences, in emotional states, in humour, our relationships with others, and in our stages of transition. We have to be careful that our strong sense of group does not create a consensus or set of values that act to police what is said and done.

We noted that relationships and hierarchies from outside the group have been imported into the group. Friendships that existed before the group was formed were significant in our early relationships with each other. Some friendships go back decades, others are built on joint work over a number of years. These have created different ties, but not prevented new and rich ones from forming. The stage of retirement has also created some new differences between us. Those of us with the longest time before retirement have sometimes had to assert our places in the group.

Hierarchical relationships from our employing organisation have also to some extent been imported. Diana comments on the licence we may have afforded her, because she is a professor. She might have been better served by more challenge. Another significant difference, and occasional tension, has been that some of us have partners and others do not. Some of us live alone. We are not all heterosexual. Some of us have grandchildren. Some of us have responsibility for dogs. These differences have influenced how some members feel they can act with others and what they feel is allowed in the group. We work at not making dissent and differences uncomfortable.

We note too that getting a balance for each individual between challenge and support is a delicate matter. This too develops over time as trust grows, by being open to challenge and by challenging.

Such matters have occasionally been painful to expose, but our periodic reviews help build awareness and continued trust. We also acknowledge the value of humour and of the shared social activities of our group in these processes.

### Mundane but important matters

These include arranging dates, which gets more and more difficult as fewer and fewer of us are employed in our institution. It also means organising someone to book a room, to bring refreshments, to tell the absentees what we did and what we have planned for the future. In arranging our residential weekends, someone has to find a good place, make reservations and organise the facilities, while taking account of our different tastes and funds. We have had to take account of cost and affordability for our activities, especially for residential events.

We keep in good touch, especially by email. We often send group emails containing useful information, about events some of us might attend, snippets such as poems, details of books or articles, humorous anecdotes and of course details of our own meetings. This has been important in keeping in touch with women who can't attend the monthly meeting.

### Agreeing activities

We have had to discuss how we run our sessions. Usually we give each person attending a share of time to report on their progress and to explore anything they want to share with the group. Sometimes we have agreed in advance to focus on a particular theme, such as paying attention to our health as we get older, or the rituals of farewells.

To date we have reviewed our individual progress and set new goals for our retiring lives annually. We always try to find ways to be supportive of each other, for example through questioning, recommending resources (such as books or processes that we have found helpful) and volunteering to support someone with a particular target or task in some practical way. The monthly meetings can include updating on progress towards a particular objective or towards the kind of life we want to lead.

We used an external facilitator on our first residential event. The consensus is that our group was greatly assisted by her at the start, but since then we have not felt it was necessary to have external facilitation. We have not decided that we can't use expertise from outside the group, but have only done this on one other occasion. In an early session we asked a recently retired colleague, Anne Peters, to tell us about her experience of retiring. She was still in transition and as her experience was so valuable, and as she expressed a need to explore it further, so she became the eighth and final member of our group. Our occasional attempts to find a health expert have not yet been successful.

## Concluding thoughts

In conclusion, we think that the following factors have helped us to work in and through the group:

All our members have significant experience of working in teams and working through teams. We share some important knowledge and experiences about how groups can work, and this is used explicitly within the group.

We share some important values about working with others, which means that, as far as we can, decisions are discussed and differences respected and accommodated.

We also have strong social connections within the group. All of us had people we count as friends among the members when we joined the group. Many of these had been established over many years, even decades. The group has developed its social cohesion through the residential weekends, through shared (but not exclusive) activities such as walking together, dining, sharing experiences of books, films, writing and numerous other valuable bits of information (poems, recipes, underwear shops, websites and so forth) and – everyone's favourite – cocktails.

This group's development, while centred on our experiences of retiring, has been organic, not forced, nor restrained. Some of the spin-offs have involved other people and activities not directly linked with retiring. These include the Vegetarian Circle, a stitching group, this book, and some workshops for former colleagues considering retiring.

We do not know what the future will hold for the group. We think that groups need to change over time if they are to continue to serve their purposes, and we do not like to think that the group will just fizzle out. We will continue to check out whether we think the group should end or not. At the moment we are all finding it an important community in our changing lives.

# Section 2
# **Retiring stories**

In this section we present different ways of seeing and experiencing the retiring process. Each contributor tells their story of retiring and what they are learning. No two stories are similar. It is striking how different their stories are, not just in their foci but in the way they approach the storytelling. While each story features a number of different dimensions there are some overarching themes. The men and women who have considered retiring are at various stages in the process, ranging from still being employed on a part-time basis to being fully retired for several years.

**Teacher's Christmas**
by Ursula Fanthorpe

*It's not so much whose cards don't come,*
*Friends of one's parents, old distinguished colleagues*
*Who taught the colonies and, retiring home,*
*Did a spot of dignified coaching. Their sudden silence*
*Is a well-bred withdrawing, not unexpected.*

*But those whose move from address to more sheltered address,*
*Whose writing gutters gently year by year,*
*Whose still hoping to see you again after love*
*Is bluff; or those who write after Christmas*
*Because cards are so expensive now. Ah those, how those*

*Punctiliously chart their long decline.*

*The stages grow familiar, like disease.*
*First it's my dauntless mini, less staunch now,*
But I could come by bus, with sandwiches.
I shall enjoy the jaunt.

*WEA classes go. Then television*
*Becomes remote, and radio's*
*For the hard of hearing. Still they write,*
*They write at Christmas. Prithee, good death's-heads,*
*Bid me not remember mine end.*

*Season as well of cards from brilliant girls,*
*A little less incisive every year,*
*Reporting comings, goings: another Hannah,*
*Another Jamie; another husband going off; and*
Writing my thesis is like digging a well with a pin.

*You, the storm-troopers of a newer, better world.*

*Down with you, holly. Come down, ivy.*

Reprinted from *A Watching Brief*,
published by Peterloo Poets.

# Chapter 4

# Three teachers talk about retiring

## Barbara Patilla, Anne Freeman and Lorna Hoey

*'I'm retired – goodbye tension, hello pension.'*

Anon.

In this chapter, Barbara, Anne and Lorna talk about their experiences of retiring from a career in teaching in secondary schools and a further education college. The three contributors know each other as they once taught in the same school. They are still friends and meet regularly as part of a walking group.

Barbara examines her last years of teaching and early days of retiring through an analysis of her dreams and diary entries. She comes to realise that endings provoke powerful feelings that need to be acknowledged and discussed in order to move on and make a new start. Selling her house is a big factor in her life – an emotional roller coaster.

Anne reflects on her transitions in the last 14 months of retiring. She discusses the satisfactions of working life and some frustrations and considers how the latter helped her in making the decision to retire. She is excited about the changes in her new life, the varied projects she has begun and the idea of developing something completely new.

Lorna identifies mistaken assumptions from others about her feelings and is not apologising for being joyful in retirement. She reflects on people's attitudes about the way she has lived her life and, in their eyes, how fortunate she has been. Lorna also talks about what she misses and doesn't miss about working life. She reports on successes in fulfilling lifelong dreams.

### Barbara Patilla: a teacher in transition

My decision to retire at the age of 61 was planned to give me time to start a new life before getting too old to want to move or change.

What are you going to do? people asked. I wasn't sure and knew that the first few months of retirement might be spent making decisions. I started keeping a diary of how I was feeling, including thoughts I had about the next phase in life's journey.

I was lucky to have had transitions in school over the previous five years that made leaving easier. My main role in the school was as head of year; a job I had for 14 years. I then became research co-ordinator in the school and took over management of Biology A level teaching. In my last two years I moved from main school teaching Science and Biology and taught only in the sixth form vocational faculty. My real passions in teaching were the pastoral care and Biology.

Only two months into 'being retired' I realise that I did need time for the process of sorting out my priorities for the future. Much of the two months has been taken up with sorting out what to do with a house that I have co-owned for 16 years and has to be sold. That has been more of an emotional roller coaster than any feelings about retirement.

I started having vivid dreams and decided to record them in order to make sense of my feelings.

In the last two weeks of school I had a dream where I was inside a spaceship – like in one of the recent *Dr Who* episodes. When the door opened I would be sucked out into oblivion. I lay by this door feeling calm and waiting for the end.

One explanation for this is that it has to do with the way in which I cope with endings sometimes. I cut off the feelings and don't face up to the loss. I think of it as 'calm' but there are no feelings there. I will be leaving my work which I have enjoyed and will be selling my home that I love.

This is a time for having feelings and working out what they mean for me. Examining my diary entries has helped me do this:

*Diary note, 22/09/08*
*Find that now I am retired I have lots of time to fill. Today I saw an estate agent here at home and then went to my Yoga class. Came back and have done some singing practice and reading, but still feel I have a gap. I think it's because I am still in limbo.*

This limbo state is described in an earlier diary entry:

*Diary note, 21/08/08 10pm*
*Tonight for the first time I feel anxiety/fear? I feel in Limbo. I think it*
*feels sad more than anything else. I have lost something very important*
*to me. Identifying this makes me feel sad.*

My diary continues in a reflective way, noting the strong feelings aroused by
the loss and change:

*What is different about today from all the saying goodbye days? Today*
*is exam results day and I went into school. I went into my email to send*
*a message to a colleague asking for some feedback from moderators as*
*to whether they had changed my marking – ever the professional. In my*
*Inbox I find two emails from students sharing their success in a retake*
*exam and thanking me for my support. They know I have left and say*
*they will miss me.*

I realise that it is the students that I will miss. Teaching them was a challenge
but they always gave me validation as a teacher.

*Also today I have visited a colleague and friend in hospital who retired*
*last year. She reinforced for me how strange it is to not be busy planning*
*for the coming year. Getting the pens and new diaries and planning*
*sheets. What pleasure I got from this purposeful activity.*

Do I now need to find a purpose? What is my identity if not a teacher? Do
I need to feel useful?

*I realise this week that I have been in denial about the move and sale of*
*the house. All my discourse with friends has been around how selling*
*the house makes sense and I have clung to straws on my retirement*
*cards that say 'One door closes and another one opens'. I have even*
*had excited moments looking at what I could rent or buy and financial*
*consultants have helped me be realistic about options.*

It strikes me that I really am scared about the future.

*Diary note, 27/08/08*
*I had strange dreams last night. The first was about school. There were*
*some people in who wanted to do interviews with staff and pupils. I*
*went to the meeting room but the time was inconvenient as I explained*
*that I had to teach a Year 8 class. When I was at the interview room*
*there were lots of pupils there who were unsupervised. Some were*

*truanting from their lessons as their appointment times on their cards
were different. I organised them and then told the men doing the
interviews that I could not come back until 3.30pm to be interviewed.
An appointment I didn't make because I was too busy.*

Considering this dream evoked feelings that I would have had this better
organised. When I remember my organisational abilities as a head of year I
knew this would be the case. This has been a recurring theme over the past two
years in work where I downsized from a responsible position but clearly (in
retrospect) missed being in charge while, at the same time, saying it was nice
not to have the stress of such responsibility!

*Diary note, 30/08/08*
*I am on the train to Devon for a walking holiday so that I am out of
London when school starts. I am listening to Brahms Violin Concerto.*

*Diary note, 31/08/08*
*Dreams before starting school at the beginning of the year are
something that I have always had but I am surprised to have them last
night since I am on holiday. Wake in one dream at 6.15am.
I had a lesson with 6th form doing an Art course. I asked them to make
a poster on black paper. (Strange dream as I am a Science teacher and
have never taught Art.)*

*One student finished her work and I am putting this up on blue
background paper that has been on the wall for ages.*

*At the end of the lesson I want to speak to the group to ask them to
finish the work for homework and make a title. Another, younger, class
comes in to register with their teacher at the end of the day – in another
part of the room but in the same large Art space, so it takes ages to
convey the information. I am feeling pleased that the students have done
some good work.*

*On leaving school I meet someone who tells me that the Art teacher
in school is angry and almost crying. I then meet her as she is leaving
school. I explain that I haven't had time to plan the whole scheme of
work so did a one-off starter. She gets angry and talks about personal
stuff – seeing her Mum – then uses language to describe assessment of
this group and the 'vertiginous dimensions' being 15% of the marks and
this is the problem with my lesson.*

*I explain that I haven't had the scheme of work over the holidays and wanted to do the planning with her because I haven't worked in the Art department before and I need materials for my displays.*
*WAKE UP here in frustration and record the dream even though it makes no sense to me. The language I remember from the dream certainly makes me dizzy!*

These strange and powerful dreams and diary notes convey to me how affected I was at the loss of my important role and the confusion about finding an identity, purpose in my life and new home.

I am now feeling more sure about my priorities for the future. Music has played an important part of my retirement. I write this as I listen to a very affirmative Piano Trio by Schubert. I am doing lots of singing with different choral groups and I go to two classes with an inspirational music teacher. Two hours in the middle of the day, what a luxury, and I have time to read about the composers and listen to their music. There are so many courses at the adult learning centres. I will never be short of things to do. I have classes on every day of the week except my day off on Wednesday. I do Pilates and Yoga. Without this structure, after such a structured job, I think I would feel lost. It also gets me out of the house.

I am still organising the walking group of friends from my old school. I can now go to ballet, music and theatre mid-week because I don't have to get out of bed before sunrise. The house is still on the market but I have seen a few places nearby that I could buy that would give me all I need in a home.

The future looks bright and my diary seems very full with all the things that I have chosen to do.

### Anne Freeman: thoughts on retirement from the perspective of a teacher now retired for 14 months

For several years I had begun to feel that work had practically taken over my life so decided to retire at 60. I would have been happy to stay until 65 but the job of teaching and in my case running a large Design and Technology Faculty was too demanding physically, intellectually and emotionally. I knew I didn't have the stamina to carry on and do the job as effectively as it should be done.

Financially, in preparation for retirement I had already decided that with any spare money I had I would pay off the mortgage with higher monthly repayments. I would advise anyone to do this. For the last two years I reduced my time to 0.8. Having investigated how this would affect my pension I found it to be worth the minimal loss of pension I incurred. This worked to some extent but I still found I spent my day off doing 'school work'! Sorting out how much money you will have in retirement is very important; I am still able to live the sort of lifestyle I had prior to retirement. I feel that my quality of life would be very different if I had to think about money every time I went to an exhibition, out for a meal or on holiday.

What would I do all day? Having had a period of time off in my thirties through a serious illness I knew just how long a day can be with nothing to do. I have a lot of interests so was looking forward to pursuing those but was concerned at how I would cope with a lot of time on my hands.

To this end and to ease myself gently into full retirement, I decided to do some supply teaching two days a week with a thought to getting a very part-time teaching job locally. I was also appointed to a post as a sessional lecturer for one session a week teaching basic gardening to adults with special needs. Gardening has always been one of my main interests.

Supply teaching was very interesting especially visiting many different schools, teaching boys for the first time in 18 years, not being in an inner-city school and seeing the different facilities available in each school. I enjoyed this for a while, especially leaving at 3.30 p.m. with no preparation or marking! But in the end this was not very satisfying as I never saw the progress students made and didn't feel part of the school community. I enjoyed teaching the gardening skills course very much but due to a college amalgamation and new rules governing funding of work-related courses this course closed in September.

What do I miss? The school community; most of the staff I worked with; being part of something that contributed to society; feeling that I was doing something important; the response of the students to my teaching and caring about them; helping students to achieve their very best and gain some self-esteem; and, finally, working with a subject that I love.

What don't I miss? Getting up at 5.40 a.m. every weekday; dealing with difficult staff (definitely more of a problem than the students); never feeling that I could fully relax even at weekends; rationing my social and family life as I always had schoolwork to do.

Not having to deal with these problems has been sheer bliss but it's taken me a year to let go of the feeling 'I'm sure I should be doing something'.

Now that I am fully retired I am enjoying myself so much. This to some extent has surprised me. I think I was a little scared of having so much time on my hands after working for so many years. I now feel completely free and am relishing the feeling. I can respond to social and family requests without working out if I can spare the time. Now my problem is 'Have I got a space in my diary?'

I did a course on Photoshop in the first term which has led to my spending lots of time working on my photographs and putting them on the Internet site Flickr for others to share. I have taken photos of the sunset from the bottom of my garden since January and am going to complete a whole year of this with a view to making a montage of the photos. I have been taking photos of the plants in my garden since January so that I have a record of a year. This has meant that my daughter in Vancouver can keep in touch with how the garden is progressing. She now has her own garden and has become interested in gardening.

I have produced some textile work to my own designs for the house and am starting on more designs this winter when I can't get outside in the garden. I have lots of time to read and feel no guilt when I sit down for a couple of hours on a sunny afternoon in the garden or rainy day indoors reading for pleasure. I can watch *Question Time* late on Thursday knowing that I don't have to get up at 5.40 a.m. I can spend all day in the garden just pottering rather than only doing what is absolutely necessary. I am enjoying walking, especially with a group from my old school. Since my husband retired this year I am also enjoying decorating and refurbishing our bedroom and bathroom with him, not done since 1986. I am enjoying going on holidays in term time. The free bus pass is fantastic, no paying for car parks or driving round looking for one. I always enjoyed cooking but now I have time to try out new dishes and make chutneys, jams, bread and other time-consuming products.

So what do I see myself doing in the future? At this moment, I feel the last year and the immediate future to be very much 'me' time. I do have the need to find something where I feel I am actually contributing to society again. My initial thoughts are something to do with nature conservation, perhaps joining a local group, doing a course on the environment or a related subject. Maybe I will find something completely new that I become interested in. That's the joy of being retired.

Would I go back to work? NO.

## Lorna Hoey: retirement

No.
I refuse to apologise.
'Don't you miss your colleagues?' friends ask.
No.
'Well – surely you miss the pupils?'
Well, actually, no.
'The hustle and bustle of the working life?'
Absolutely not.
'The gossip in the staffroom?'
Yeuchhh.
'You were a senior manager. What about the status?'
Never.

And none of these are the right answer. Instead, I'm expected to say, Yes, I miss everyone, I think about my ex-pupils constantly; I miss those Fridays in the pub when my colleagues and I thrashed out the week over a few pints in the glorious, reckless knowledge that the next day was a Saturday. Yes, I'm expected to say, my life is so quiet now, so purposeless and of course it was such a noble profession to be part of (remember that *if you can read this, thank a teacher* sticker?) and I miss the discipline, the days divided into 50-minute chunks by a string of bleeps, oh, maybe I should find a hobby…

No. Sorry – but I'm not apologising, you understand? I'm joyful.

Suddenly I'm free.

I got so tired of having to say sorry.

First it was because I was a 'baby boomer'. Apparently, we'd never had it so good. Then it was about being the 'have-it-all' generation. Then it was about student grants, the hand-out mortgages, the top-ups and loans there for the asking.

Not to mention being a Sixties chick. We didn't dress like our mothers. We didn't think like our mothers. And we bought – oh boy, we bought – boots and Biba and singles and EPs and sometimes LPs – to 'spin' on the Dansette.

Aren't you lucky, everyone said. We never had those chances. We had to fight in a war. Yes, I said. Sorry.

We were the Bulge Generation. There were more of us around than there had ever been, in any generation, so we were told. And it was true – hadn't we sat three to a desk in a space made for two? Hadn't we fought for our portions of school dinner because there clearly wasn't enough for everybody?

We were told we were part of the greatest period of economic growth since the war. We had responsibility. We went to university. We saved up for the passport fee and went travelling, saying goodbye to parents for months on end and leaving them without benefit of mobile phones or emails. And somehow they let us go. We were the new generation, forging ahead, carving out new paths, new ways of thinking and juggling careers with looking after baby.

We job-shared. In my profession, teaching, we didn't have to pack it in when we got married, as my aunt had to do in 1940. We wore our demure skirts for work, and our thigh boots with hot-pants at the weekend, and we worked as hard as the male colleagues in the staffroom and maybe more, who knows? – yet, as females, we were paid less. My in-service record as an Art teacher for 1971 will read 'Gross Misconduct' for I was severely reprimanded for wearing trousers, even though as a painter of school scenery for the annual 'production', my work involved clambering about on scaffolding and perching on ladders.

'You've got some great stories,' they say. 'Surely,' they intone hopefully, 'surely, you must miss all that?'

Why?

I'm still sharing pints with colleagues from my first school, my fifth school, my eleventh school, my last school. And I'm still telling my stories on email, blog and Skype to colleagues who are now on the other side of the world. I'm going to concerts and demonstrations and writing groups and walking groups with colleagues who have become dear friends.

I'm still waking at six, but I can lie still and listen to the traffic in the street outside and know that I don't need to be part of it any more. Never again will I scrape an icy windscreen at 7 a.m. No longer will I cram myself onto a Tube with a thousand scowling others, none of us wishing to be there. I can enjoy the whole of a weekend, not just Saturday and Sunday morning but every bit of it. The black cloud won't descend mid-Sunday afternoon when I think, automatically, *Who am I teaching tomorrow? What am I teaching tomorrow? Have I marked their books?* And the inevitable, *What am I going to wear?*

The holidays are real holidays. (*'Oh, but you teachers, you get all those holidays....'*) I spent every Easter holiday running revision classes and assessing GCSE coursework folders. The first part of the summer holiday was spent in school, tidying out my classroom and putting up new posters. I managed two, maybe three weeks clear holiday space, to get to know my family again. The last week of the 'summer holidays' was spent in school preparing lessons, nervous about the new term. Christmas was a flurry of present-buying and cooking, everything crammed into ten days or so. The half-terms were often spent in bed with some ailment as the body caved in, demanding attention.

Now my husband and I can choose to have a holiday, or not. We can go in the middle of the term, in the middle of the week, in the middle of the night. We can stay for as long as money and family commitments allow. But we are not bound by work.

Sure, we are restricted by that hedge-fund manager's breakfast of choice, Credit Crunch. Now we make a proper shopping list for Tesco's and, generally, stick to it. I've cut up a few old suits and dyed a jacket and hope that I'm not invited to any posh parties soon as I've nothing, really nothing, to wear. I can't impulse-buy that lipstick and my hair is coloured out of a packet from a chemist's in N4, rather than costing a packet from a glitzy establishment in W1.

But I'm free, and I've got the Freedom Pass to prove it. The best thing that ever happened to pensioners, this little orange pouch carries me all around London for nothing at all. Yes, I see those glares. I know, I know, you have to put a fortune on your Oyster every month, and I don't. Sorry. Well, not really.

At last there's the time to do the things I dreamed about – and that's what it's all about. There's time to write the novel (yes, I'm doing it) and time to finish my model of a Moroccan house (yes, doing that too) and to eat a healthy diet and to meet my friends and to read my way through the Booker Prize shortlist and oh, just do stuff for the hell of it like – dance around to my iPod, scuffle leaves in the park, knit a tree (yes, I've done that).

Don't get me wrong. I've loved my life so far. I still read the *TES* and wonder about the demise of SATs and worry about the new Diplomas. But I don't really feel part of it any more. I've done it, really. I'm ready for the next phase, starting now.

And no, I don't miss all the things I've done, the schools I've worked in, the projects I've been involved in, the clever, funny, inspiring pupils and colleagues that I've known. But it's time to move on.

Sorry.

Well, no, actually, I'm not.

Chapter 5

# Hip-hop, illness and early retirement

## Gil Bennet

*'In every change is an opportunity.'*

Hugh Wiley

> Gil retired early from the demanding post of deputy headteacher in a sec-
> ondary school in Newcastle, unintentionally and without plans, as a result
> of physical problems. Her story is one of discovery: of depression as a result
> of pain and a complex response to leaving work unexpectedly; of finding
> some resources within herself to combat depression and physical problems;
> of strategies to achieve her goals; and of new skills and delights now she
> has recovered. It could have been a sad story, but Gil has ensured retiring
> has brought her adventures and possibilities.

At 49 I had no idea of taking early retirement. It had never entered my head.
I was happy in the job I was doing, felt youthful and healthy; retirement was
in the very dim and distant future. I was a deputy headteacher in an inner-city
comprehensive school in Newcastle upon Tyne. Not much time for contem-
plation and retirees were often cynical colleagues who sat in corners of the
staffroom muttering about how much better education was in the good old
days and how they couldn't wait to get out on the golf course instead of wasting time with the adolescent young. I was NOT one of them. I had plenty to
interest me in education. I was involved in lots of in-service training for my
local authority, I was chair of the National Association for Pastoral Care in
Education and I was on the advisory committee of the British Board of Film
Classification in London. I also liked the contact I had with young people and
still felt enthusiastic about classroom teaching.

However, not everything stays the same. I was looking to change jobs. Perhaps I should go for a headship? The challenge of another deputy's job in a school elsewhere in the country was interesting. For family reasons my home in the North East was beginning to be less attractive. My children had both left the area and were living in London and I also had a small granddaughter there. My parents were becoming more frail and less able to travel from Oxford to visit me. My brother was in Oxford, my sister in Cambridge. Since my marriage had ended I was almost 300 miles from my nearest family member and visited the South East frequently. Certainly I was in the South every holiday. I spent too much time on the motorway. The year I was 49 I was looking for other jobs elsewhere in the country and change was going to happen.

I was on summer holiday in Greece when the unexpected happened. It was August and the island was idyllic. I woke one morning halfway through the holiday with a pain in my hip. There had been no sprain as far as I could remember and as I limped into the sunshine I confidently expected that the pain would diminish during the day. It got worse. I have always been fairly fit. I have never run a marathon but I exercised frequently, walked in the Northumbrian countryside most weekends and swam 50 lengths of the school pool every Friday. Suddenly swimming breaststroke was painful. After a few lengths I had to stop. Walking, equally, was not the pleasure it had been. I determined to see a GP as soon as I got home and was certain that this was a temporary setback that would be sorted out quickly. After all, one expects one's body to work. It always has done. How can things suddenly change without warning? There had been some warnings, of course. I had visited my doctor a month earlier complaining of an intermittent sharp pain down my right thigh. He dismissed it as unimportant and suggested I increase my exercise regime. The pain became my constant companion for the next rather dark months while the medics tried to work out why a fit, healthy woman should suddenly experience the kind of problems usually not seen until 30 years later. It took a further six months and an exploratory operation to identify the problem, with phrases like 'bone cancer', 'tuberculosis of the bone' and eventually, much later 'total hip replacement' becoming part of my consciousness.

At the end of the summer holiday I returned to work expecting that a cause and a cure were close. My world suddenly became smaller. I could no longer walk from home to the centre of the city to visit the cinema. I had to think hard about how to get from place to place. The job became more difficult as bounding up three flights of stairs was no longer possible and break/dinner duty became a torture. My car was vital and easy parking places were like gold. By the end of each day I was physically exhausted. I started to think more about what was important in my life and the most important thing was not necessarily the job. Intimations of mortality concentrate the mind and if my physical freedom was circumscribed I wanted more choices than I felt I had.

During the autumn term the school had some hard decisions to make. The East end of Newcastle was in the middle of big demographic changes and school rolls were falling. During the previous school year two members of staff were redeployed to schools in burgeoning parts of the city, a painful process in which I had been closely involved. We still needed to make budgetary savings if our books were to balance in the future. Staff costs are always the largest part of any school budget and losing staff when student numbers are falling is the best alternative. We could not rely on natural wastage. Our staff had always been pretty stable and the whole of the North East was suffering from falling rolls. The head and three deputies had all been appointed when the school was larger and our salaries reflected that. We were a huge drain on the budget and not every member of staff thought we were worth the money. I was in charge of finance. We needed to lose a deputy headteacher. I was almost 50. The local education authority had put together very tempting redundancy packages. Suddenly I began to think the unthinkable. I could retire. I limped home that night with a great deal to think about.

I had no retirement plan and no idea how I would fill the huge void left by teaching, but already work was becoming more problematic. I didn't know how long I could continue in the job anyway. At this stage my physical problems had not been diagnosed and my day-to-day regime was increasingly hard. I had to take time off to visit specialists and when in January I slipped on packed ice and fell awkwardly to protect my hip, I managed to break my wrist. Now I could neither walk nor drive for six weeks. I was becoming a liability at work. I decided to request early retirement. After all, I could always change my mind.

As I started to explore the possibility of ending my teaching career there were a number of criteria that I decided were important to me if I was to take this rather extraordinary step. If I were to leave the job I enjoyed I wanted to do something entirely different. I was not ready to be known as a 'retired teacher from Benfield School' for the rest of my life. Since the Inspectorate was less to do with development and more to do with assessment I was not interested in that popular route. I could always do supply teaching to augment an income of less than half the one I was used to. First, I would move and the only place for me was London (if it didn't work out I could always come back). Second, there were other fields I wanted to explore, perhaps writing fiction, perhaps becoming a Justice of the Peace, perhaps doing a research degree, certainly travelling outside school holidays. The world began to seem to have other possibilities until I remembered the reason I was considering leaving was because I couldn't even do this job properly. I had a disability, perhaps curable, perhaps not, but the idea of changing my life had presented itself and taken hold. I put in my application for voluntary redundancy/early retirement and had it accepted. I would finish my teaching career the following summer.

Here is the sad part of my story. That plan had to be modified. Pain had become a permanent part of my life and painkillers didn't seem to help. I struggled to do the job but increasingly I was getting home from work so exhausted that I could barely manage to cook supper. Eventually one evening I looked in the mirror when I got home and my face was pale green. I went straight to bed without eating and next morning, defeated, I rang the school to say I was unable to do the job. I never went back. I retired without preparation or strategy, without support and before I was ready. Not a good idea. Suddenly I had no role to fulfill and no purpose to my days. The status I had enjoyed as deputy head was withdrawn. Worse, I left projects unfinished, with tasks begun and left in a mess. When the end came it came so quickly I had no time to complete anything. I never returned, apart from a visit on crutches to say goodbye at the end of term meeting and a later visit to clear my desk. Not a good idea.

My friends and colleagues all still had busy lives and although sympathetic, they rather envied my empty days. I felt I was letting my colleagues down, a fraud. I looked quite as usual when I didn't try to walk, even fit and healthy, but my life was far from normal. I felt useless and incapable. I burst into tears if anyone enquired about my health and spent days just sitting feeling miserable, hardly able to move from the sofa, and very alone. I tried to hide my depression from everyone and felt ashamed that I was so feeble. I was unable to plan for a future that seemed very uncertain and my resources were used up combating the pain that only went away if I sat quietly doing nothing. I was in limbo with everything on hold.

Actually I was extremely lucky because there was a way out. The diagnosis, when it came after many delays, came with a solution. I had osteoarthritis in one hip, probably because of degeneration following a car accident some 20 years earlier, and a full hip replacement operation would most probably cure the problem. There was a 6–12-month waiting list for the operation but the prospect of getting back to a pain-free existence gave me something to work towards. I realised that the inactivity I had allowed to become my norm was not going to help me recover after the operation. I needed to find some way to get fit again. I couldn't walk but I could cycle for short distances. I bought a bike. A friend lent me an exercise bike and I set myself to build up the muscles that had been wasting and that I hoped I would need after a successful operation. I made sure that every day I exercised with the bike for at least 40 minutes. This physical activity helped my psychological state and I began to explore possibilities for using my time more creatively.

Even at my most depressed I had never allowed myself to get sucked into watching daytime television or staying in bed until lunchtime and now I began to develop a rough timetable for my days. I still felt incapable of doing anything work-related. I shoved the thought of writing or drawing away. I started to do needlepoint. It sounds very genteel and old ladyish but I managed to find some edgy ready-made designs and began to embroider. This repetitive and gentle activity seemed to allow some kind of healing to take place. I have never done any of this work since, but I do have six very fetching cushions, two of which I designed myself. I also began to visit the library, on my bike, and set myself to read all the books I had wanted to but never had time for. Living for some of each day in a world of fiction again helped my emotional convalescence.

The other project I set myself was to try to get the operation date fixed. I discovered quite a lot about the National Health Service. First, I got to know my local hospital bed manager by name and kept in touch. Administrators often don't have enough contact with their clients; they like to help and will try to do so. I telephoned every week. I also made arrangements so that I could go into hospital at a moment's notice. If there are any cancellations it is very useful to have someone available to fill the place and if someone has just called up for a chat then that someone's name springs to mind to fill the gap. With goals in mind, although with a very different lifestyle, depression began to lift and the operation was the star on my horizon.

As with the onset of the problem and the need to stop work the appointment to go into hospital came suddenly. There was a cancellation and towards the end of June I finally went into the operating theatre. As soon as I was allowed out of bed afterwards I realised that, although I was sore and weak, the pain when I put my foot to the ground was gone. Immediately the resolve to pick up my life again came back. Energy was slower to return but every day made a difference. I had achievable goals. They were things like learning to climb stairs safely with two crutches, putting socks on without bending the knees, walking again. Each goal achieved spurred me to try harder and increased my cheerfulness. My colleagues came in droves to visit me in hospital and I felt vindicated in being away from work; the medical imperatives were obvious so I felt less guilty. I could begin to take charge of my life again and start to think about plans for the future.

The convalescent period lasted a few months and my doctors refused to allow me back to work until after my early retirement date came and went. The depression that hit me when I stopped working never returned and subsequently my life entered phases it would not have done had I continued in the job I was doing. I returned to my first love as a ceramics designer, something I didn't realise I wanted to do until I began to dream about making large pots and signed up for a daytime pottery class. I moved to London and renovated a flat. I completed a City and Guilds qualification in ceramics and had a ceramics studio built in the garden. I discovered I could still hack it in the classroom by doing supply teaching all over London. I discovered travel to other cultures and have backpacked to different continents. Most surprisingly of all I met and married a new partner a little after a year of moving south.

I think that the experience of disability made me learn different ways of responding to problems. I am much more sensitive if people have medical issues. Before this experience I had the fit, healthy person's private and hidden belief that illness is somehow brought on by feebleness or some other lack of virtue and can be dealt with if only the will is there. Fifty years ago, before advances in orthopaedic surgery I would have been in a wheelchair for the rest of my life.

I became more open to opportunities that present themselves and less hidebound by expectations, my own and those of others. I still sometimes regret not having taken my teaching career further. I did not fulfill my whole potential there but the very different life I have led since I was 50 and took early retirement has brought adventures and possibilities I could not have imagined. The regrets are few and the satisfactions are many.

Chapter 6

# Transitions and transformations

## Eileen Carnell

*'There's never enough time to do all the nothing you want.'*
                                                    Bill Watterson

This story is about Eileen's insights into viewing retiring as a series of transitions and transformations as she struggles to find new identities. She describes a positive new lifestyle in which she has come to realise the importance of paying attention to the physical, emotional, intellectual, social and personal dimensions of retiring. Eileen highlights her learning along the way especially to do with what has helped and hindered her progress. Despite unexpected setbacks and periods of discomfort and stress she is beginning to achieve a new sense of herself. She is developing a rhythm to her life that embraces the many activities, personal perspectives, relationships and networks that are important in making her life fulfilling, challenging and happy.

I love my new life and my newly developing identity as a retiring person. I love the freedom and the sense that I can do anything. I love having the energy to pursue a whole range of activities, to go out every evening mid-week without a care, go to bed late and get up whenever I feel like it. I am extremely optimistic about the future and I feel I am developing a relationship with a new me.

The most important thing that I have learned is that retiring is an active process – a series of transitions and transformations.

### Transitions – problematic or liberating?

I have learned through personal experiences and research that transitions in any area of life and at any age can be problematic and lengthy processes. These processes include adapting to new ways of being, new ways of seeing things and developing different perspectives. There are also issues around gaining access to new experiences and networks. I have also learned that transitions can be liberating and exciting. The difference between these positive and negative positions may relate to one's attitude towards the transition, whether the transition is freely chosen or forced, how much preparation has been done and how willing a person is to learn and change.

My story examines how I have learnt to adapt to a new way of being, and what I have had to learn, and unlearn, on the way. I want to draw out issues around my changing expectations and changing emotions in shifting from fully employed to working part-time initially and then working on a consultancy basis. I want to look at the key relationships that have supported my transitions and the effects of transitions on my social, professional and personal identities. I also look at my perceptions of the effects of my changes on my partner and friends. Many factors seem to help or hinder the processes of transition, and I want in particular to draw out the significance of learning transformations, and the various forms these may take and what has supported me in the process.

### The beginning of my retiring journey

My story starts six years ago and since then I have been planning and preparing to retire. In January 2002 when I had my fifty-fifth birthday I was sent, along with everybody in the organisation aged 55 or over, a letter to ask if I wanted to take early retirement. I jumped at the chance, thinking about all the other things I wanted to do, including other paid work. I wanted the chance to live a different sort of life, not tied to an organisation as I had been all my working life. I became excited at the prospect and began making plans, sorted out my finances, including putting different pots of money into one pension fund. This took an amazing amount of time and trouble. I was helped by a really good independent financial adviser (see Chapter 17). However, it was not to be. Six months after I applied I heard that my application had been refused. I was disappointed but not heartbroken as I enjoyed my work, especially collaborating with special colleagues. This unexpected setback coincided with the death of my father, and just a month later, the death of my sister. This was a difficult time for me and for about two years I felt depressed and trapped.

As I came out of the depression I began thinking again of retiring. I started to count down the months, then weeks and then days to my sixtieth birthday and went ahead with new plans for retiring. Two experiences helped me be clear about wanting to retire. One, gaining a sense of what my life might be like if I was not tied to working in a particular organisation, and two, finding myself doing work I was not enjoying.

From this experience I learned that when things do not go exactly as planned it doesn't prevent a person getting to the place they want to be eventually.

I was glad I had sorted out my finances and saw my financial adviser again. He helped me with projections, forecasts and sorting all the paperwork that was necessary. I learned that the time taken to do these tasks should not be underestimated. It was like having another part-time job. Despite the forecasts I was not sure that my state pension and university pension would be enough. I had been a mature student and entered the teaching profession later than most people and had worked part-time for a number of years. So I decided not to leave work completely in April 2007 but to carry on with a day a week contract in a research role plus some consultancy which amounted to another day a week. So in April 2007 I changed from working full-time to around two days a week. The day a week research contract would last just one year and I could decide how long to go on with the consultancy work after that.

## A problematic period of transition

The first six months in this arrangement were not easy. I wished I had left altogether and still felt that I was working and not retired at all. There were difficult adjustments to make at work, including 'hot-desking' which meant that there was no opportunity to control the workspace. I was having to learn a new way to be social at work and to make a personal space somewhere. I then realised the importance of one's relationship with place, something I was not aware of while I was working full-time or even part-time. Not having the tools for the job I had been used to was frustrating and stressful. It was disconcerting to be in a position where I felt disconnected from the place where I had worked for 17 years, yet still had a role there. Reflecting on this now I realise that I was between identities, negotiating my way through uncertainties, and this felt very uncomfortable. However, I was found the use of a room one day a week and had access to my own computer and storage area. This made a considerable difference. I was reconnected with the place.

## Feeling supported during the problematic period of transition

There were important resources I was able to draw on during this difficult period of transition. Having time in the Retiring Women group to talk about issues and feelings was, and still is, amazingly important (see Chapters 2 and 3). The conversations I appreciated most included talk about ways of seeing oneself differently and making sense of a new kind of life. Activities where we discussed different dimensions of one's new life such as intellectual stimulation, work, friendships, and spiritual, social, emotional and political issues highlighted that a balance of activities needed to be considered. I learned that attention to these different dimensions is extremely important.

I kept a reflective diary – noting occasions when I have felt particularly happy and some occasions when things did not seem to be so good. This has helped monitor my life and helped me understand what ensures feelings of well-being. I also note from my pedometer the number of steps I walk in a day, averaging 14,000, and what food I enjoy and how much and when I have drunk alcohol. This monitoring has really helped me take care of myself and notice the conditions surrounding my changing emotions. I do not expect to monitor in this way forever but I will do so on occasions when I feel less robust than usual and/or until I feel I have established a new way of being and obliterated old, unhealthy patterns. Six sessions with a dietician really helped and I started eating far more healthily and consequently lost weight.

## Transforming my physical self

One area I am not worrying about is sustaining my commitment to Pilates and the gym. I am fortunate in living near a really good leisure centre that is resourced by the local authority. I can walk there and really feel the benefits of regular and sustained exercises of different kinds. One important factor is that the local authority subsidises the fees for people over 60. I pay £1.40 a visit rather than £6.50 and my story would not be complete without a mention of my Freedom Pass! (See Chapter 18.)

Days when I exercise leave me feeling far more alive and energetic. My tutors at the leisure centre are fabulous and, unlike many private gyms, they are local people who have permanent jobs. It is great to feel the support of professional people who take a real interest in what I am achieving. It is good to get to know these tutors well and I feel that I have good relationships with them. This makes the visits even more enjoyable and motivating. It is a great community resource and I feel part of that community. I have wondered why this dimension of my life has been so important. It strikes me that it is to do with the acknowledgement of personal achievement. Here I get genuine praise and it contrasts with the work situation where recognition of personal achievement and praise, other than from one's closest colleagues, is so rare.

## Transforming other areas of my life

I have also transformed my home. Last year the whole of the front and back and inside of my house was decorated and repaired. This meant I had an opportunity to de-clutter every room and re-hang my paintings, reorder and recycle my books, music and decorative china. I also changed the lighting, which was particularly good last winter. The house feels nice now and it has encouraged me to entertain on a regular basis – another important goal in my new life plan. My aim was to create a new way of being at home – new spaces for doing things differently and I do feel that I have achieved this already. I recognise now the importance of being really comfortable in my home – both physically and emotionally – just as I realised its importance at work. Appropriate accommodation needs to fit your lifestyle, for example a new large dining table means I can entertain guests without their feeling cramped.

## Transforming my creative self

During one Retiring Women group meeting it was suggested that I did not need an office anymore so I have changed that space to make a studio. I want to be able to leave out all my art equipment so that I can paint and draw everyday without leaving the rest of the house in a mess. Also, going to regular classes has meant that I am beginning to feel like an artist and I really enjoy watercolour painting. I am not concerned with the outcome but really love experimenting with colour and watching the reactions of the paint. I am using the paintings to inspire design for my tapestries. I have learned that this satisfies my creative self.

I feel that the process of watercolour painting has a lot to teach me about my life. If I don't try too hard to manipulate the paint the outcome is always more exciting, dynamic and alive. Becoming more spontaneous and free presents a challenge for me in shifting from a very planned, organised and regulated life to a more spontaneous and creative one. I need to let go some very established patterns of being; a way of life I have been set in for about 40 years. We have a joke in the Retiring Women group that I am planning in my diary times to be spontaneous.

## A liberating period of transition

I want to see retiring a bit like a concept that an 11-year-old pupil shared with me about his transition from one school year to another: he said it was 'a bit like mixing colours'. He saw the accumulated effects of experience mingling and creating a whole that is more exciting, dynamic and rich. His insight coincides with a useful definition I found recently: 'The ways in which people transfer knowledge and skills between different contexts and roles constitutes a transition' (Ecclestone *et al.* 2005). These observations are helpful to me as I try and make sense of my life and understand the different changes that are taking place. At the moment I am aware of all the activities I am engaged in.

I think this is my reaction to retiring – a safety net. I am still planning and not allowing much time in my life to be spontaneous. But I am aware of this and am pleased with myself when I do act spontaneously.

I have always admired the quality in others in taking on political issues, such as those colleagues and friends who work with survivors of torture and befriending families of prisoners. This is such worthwhile work. I wanted my life to have such a dimension and I recently took part in training to become a Samaritan. I draw on the skills I developed as a voluntary bereavement counsellor for several years. My work as a Samaritan gives me an important purpose. I recognise the wisdom I can bring and that I have something important to contribute. I find this work very fulfilling and I am still learning new skills.

In considering the range of activities I am involved in I think I am taking care of my health, my friendships, my social and emotional life. I am intellectually stimulated and still have some part-time consultancy work in research, coaching and writing.

My partner and close friends have interesting reactions to my new life and new identities. My partner is very supportive of my plans and now we spend more time together and really value it. Negotiating with my partner has been crucial; time to communicate about important issues and diary planning has become more important. Nearly two years ago we had our Civil Partnership ceremony after being together for ten years. This was near to the beginning of my retiring process and it is difficult to say whether the qualitative difference in our relationship is due to the Civil Partnership or to do with my retiring. My partner is ten years younger than me and continues to work full-time. She sometimes says she is jealous of my new lifestyle and sometimes feels excluded. But now that I am working less she sees the benefits for me which can also mean benefits for her too, such as an extended nurturing dimension. My friends at work find it hard sometimes when I report what I have been doing and I can see that they are also beginning to count the days till their retirement. I am more conscious now of how I talk to my friends and colleagues and am careful not to overdo the delights of retiring.

### Some remaining tensions and struggles

There are some things that I miss. For example the exciting dialogue when supporting someone who is completing their thesis, the thrill of being with an MA group when there is a breakthrough in our learning. But when I hear my colleagues talking about how they feel overwhelmed with marking and complaining about administration and bureaucracy I am so pleased not to have a full-time job which would take over my whole life and leave me exhausted.

I guess I will miss the extra money too. It seems a little scary to think of my savings diminishing every month. I am learning that I need to see money in a different way. As one of my retired friends says: 'This *is* the rainy day.' I think the use of money in retirement is about an attitude to life rather than a business venture. In the 12 months I have had since giving up a full-time job I have spent less time doing the figures and thought more about having a really nice time. I have not been too extravagant. But I have bought whatever I fancied, including new clothes to support my new image as a retiring woman and spent lots on holidays and trips away. This feels important in two ways. First, in rewarding myself for the many years that I worked really hard and, second, a way of enjoying life to the full.

## Being part of several communities and networks

I have rediscovered the importance of networks. It strikes me now that making regular commitments to groups of people demonstrates how one values others and oneself, belonging and engaging in a way that is important for one's self-esteem and sense of being human. I belong to a new sewing group that meets monthly, I meet friends for meals regularly, arrange special outings to the ballet. I like time on my own too and do things for the sheer sense of joy and pleasure. My *a cappella* singing group provides such fun. We meet as a group of 20 unaccompanied singers, have a great time and produce great sounds ranging from jazz to classical pieces. I can't think of anything else that provides such joy and sense of well-being. The tutor has a great sense of humour and I find laughing so therapeutic. Next year I am joining the Musicianship for Singers class, which will provide a more challenging dimension.

## My learning about transitions and transformations

This has been my story of the build-up towards and first year of retiring – a period of transitions, transformations and changes in my identity. The concept of multiple transitions was introduced to me on the first residential weekend of the Retiring Women group. And for me it has been the most significant piece of learning – retiring: a process not an event, seeing life through a new lens.

These different transitions and transformations are challenging my sense of identity as I am integrating my 'changing statuses and roles' (Epstein 1978). My new image of myself is not yet coherent. I think I have been wrestling with different images and experimenting with different narratives of a retiring person – 'a storied process' (Frank 1995). The transitions have been hard in some ways but interesting. I am learning a lot about myself as a person as I am 'reconstructing' and 'navigating' my way to a new identity (Ecclestone *et al.* 2005).

One of the struggles of change of identity is the shift from being a successful academic which has defined what I did and who I was. One important example of navigating a way to a new identity is when introducing oneself to new people. Members of the Retiring Women group talk of others' eyes glazing over when in answer to the question 'What do you do?' they hear 'I'm retired.' I have found that practising new ways of talking about myself as a retiring person helps me try on new identities. Now the answer to the same question: a writer, I am writing a book on retiring; an artist, I am meeting the challenges of watercolour painting in my new free time; a singer, I sing with an *a capella* group, and so on.

Retiring has had a dramatic effect on my social, learning, professional, political and personal identities. I have been helped to understand this by two things: (1) engaging in dialogue about what retiring means and making this learning explicit, both by talk and also by reflective writing, and (2) being part of active networks and friendship groups that allow me to practise my new behaviours without judgement or criticism.

I am noticing new attitudes. I am now thinking like a person who is in the process of retiring from work and embracing a new way of being – a new way of being with myself and with other people. Two people have said to me that they felt really low when they retired. They said that they did not feel important anymore. I feel differently. I have gained a new sense of importance which may be about feeling more self-confident. I do not feel as if I have to prove anything to anyone anymore and am intrigued to see how I will develop as a retired person.

## Looking forward to future transitions and transformations

Next year presents new challenges with other transitions. From May 2008 the one day a week commitment will end. I feel good about this and look forward to more time to do other things that I have not even thought about yet.

I also want to join a local conservation group. This group meets once a week and you can just turn up whenever you feel like it. This will combine four areas of enjoyment and satisfaction – gardening, making order out of chaos, physical work and making a contribution to something lasting. I was going to volunteer to do a stint in the Galapagos after a recent trip there but realise that you can start in your own neighbourhood. Maybe I'll go back to the Galapagos in a year or two but at the moment I want to establish a life where I am retiring and finding a new way of being, not dashing about all over the world looking for big projects in order to postpone a new way of living with myself. Getting involved in a local community will also provide another social network.

Other areas in my life are even more important such as the richness of my closest, personal relationships with my partner and friends. I would not be in such a positive frame without them and I acknowledge their importance in my life. But I have focused on my transitions and transformations as this story has been about the process of my retiring and examining the opportunity to embark on a new way of seeing things as a person free from excessive work demands. Writing this story has provided me with the opportunity to explore myself as a retiring person with all the possibilities of developing a new set of identities that this allows. I am glad I am retiring. My life seems full of the things I really want to do. I feel more alive, more powerful, healthier and with a heightened sense of awareness of my personal relationships. It is a joyful period of my life.

## References

Ecclestone, K., Blackmore, T., Biesta, G., Colley, H. and Hughes, M. (2005) 'Transitions through the lifecourse: political, professional and academic perspectives'. Paper presented at the Annual TLRP/ESRC Conference, University of Warwick.

Epstein, A. (1978) *Ethos and Identity*. London: Tavistock.

Frank, A. (1995) *The Wounded Storyteller: Body, illness and ethics*. Chicago: University of Chicago Press.

# Chapter 7

# Part-time work as a way forward into retirement

## Marianne Coleman

*'When you retire, think and act as if you were still working; and when you're still working, think and act a bit as if you were already retired.'*

Anon.

In this chapter Marianne discusses a way of approaching retirement that many people are now enjoying. She examines the case for part-time work, drawing on some relevant research. She describes her own story and the reasons she came to the decision to retire in this way. She speaks of the advantages and some pitfalls of this approach, some important transitions, the necessity of being realistic about part-time commitments and the financial consequences.

If you are approaching formal retirement age, longing for the day when you can turn your back on work and move on, then retirement will be a cause for celebration. If, like me, you feel your job is worthwhile, interesting, satisfying and crucial to your identity, it seems perverse to give it up, and retirement may seem threatening. However, once you reach a certain age and stage in your life and colleagues and/or partners are making plans for retirement you tend to start thinking about some plans and decisions yourself.

At this stage in life, what are the options that are available? Recent legislation in the UK has followed the pattern of the USA to treat all workers alike regardless of age, meaning you may not have to retire at 60 or 65. However, continuing to work full-time will take a toll and there are work–life balance issues for older people that do not get recognised in the same way as those for families with young children. In Finland, in contrast to most other countries, employment policy includes an emphasis on meeting the needs of older workers, for example offering the opportunity of flexible hours and meeting occupational health issues of older people (Hirsch 2003). This is not the attitude in the UK where employers 'have done little to meet such needs' (ibid. p. 4). If you would like more flexibility in your work, and a better work–life balance, an obvious option is to change from full- to part-time work, providing of course that the work opportunities are there.

Part-time work can take many forms. It can be a structured and regular commitment covering any fraction of a normal working week, or a more flexible piecemeal arrangement such as consultancy. There may also be the possibility of job-share. About 22 per cent of the labour force work part-time in the UK (Powell and Graves 2003) and most part-timers are women. In fact 42 per cent of the female work force compared to only 9 per cent of the male workforce work part-time (Women and Work Commission 2006). Many of the women who do work part-time are those with young children and typically their skills are under-utilised and they are paid poorly. However, there are also 800,000 part-time workers among the 1.2 million people past the state pension age who are still working (Labour Force Survey 2007, quoted in DWP 2008). Of those who work past state pension age, half do so because they enjoy their work, for the remainder the main motivation is financial (DWP 2008).

To me, reducing from a full-time to a part-time work commitment seems an ideal way to 'evolve' into a state where work is no longer prioritised above other aspects of life. It has provided me with a means of preparing for retirement and coming to terms with it.

## My story

I have been a part-time worker twice. The first time was when I had young children, and the second as part of a staged retirement. At the age of 60, I moved from full-time work to a part-time contract of three days a week, and two-and-a-half years later I formally retired. I then immediately returned to work on a one-year contract for one-and-a-half days a week. The initial reduction from full-time to part-time, and then the further reduction did not immediately feel comfortable. In particular the move from full-time to three days a week took several months to get used to and initially I really missed the structure and demands of a busy full-time role. This proved to me that I was right to go to part-time as an interim step rather than fully retiring. I see moving to part-time as a stepped progression into a more flexible way of life and anticipate that the future will be more flexible still, with the possibility of just working on short-term projects interspersed with (lengthening) periods of non-working.

## *Making the decision*

I have actually made a series of interlinked decisions related to work and retirement. The first decision, which was the big one, was to move from full-time to part-time work, the second was to set a date for formal retirement and then the decision to continue working more flexibly for some years to come with my workload reducing and blending into the rest of my life.

My career profile is probably similar to many women of my age who combined a professional job with raising a family. Three years ago, approaching the state retirement age of 60 for women, I was at the peak of my career. Although I have been in paid employment more or less since university, my career progress had been limited until middle age. I had taken an enforced career break of three years when I had my first son, as it was before the days of maternity leave. Although I wanted to prioritise family commitments when my sons were young, there were very strong expectations that a woman would stay at home with children in the early 1970s and I had deeply felt the loss of status attached to being 'only' a housewife and mother. Starting again on a career after this break meant my career did not really 'take off' until I was in my late forties, so in my late fifties my career was still on an upward trajectory. At the same time I was also conscious of the landmark sixtieth birthday approaching. This mattered more than it might because my husband had already virtually retired, and although he has always been supportive of my career, we both felt that we were out of step with one another. He was free to develop new interests and we both wanted to plan for our joint future and explore travel options. In addition I was aware of being very tired and also suffering from aches and pains, particularly lower back pain. As I was getting into my car for a Saturday morning visit to the osteopath, it came to me in a flash that if I were to move to part-time work things would be a lot easier. Between opening the car door and easing myself into the seat I had actually taken a decision and it felt liberating. I did not act on it immediately, but for me the deed was done. When the opportunity presented itself at work, I mentioned that I would like to move to part-time employment and set a date for about six months later to start on my chosen three days a week.

## *Dealing with the negatives*

Although I had made a firm decision to move to part-time work, I saw this reduction as a prelude to retirement and the idea of retirement carried negative connotations and raised tensions that I had to deal with. The decision indicated that I was moving into a different part of my life as an 'old person' which I found hard to accept. I am not alone in experiencing such negative thoughts about the idea of retirement. A survey of 1,000 people over 55 indicated that on waking up on the first day of retirement 11 per cent felt 'sad', 8 per cent 'anxious' and 8 per cent 'lost' (DWP 2008). I did not move directly into retirement so did not experience the dramatic change from full work commitment to none. However, the decision to go part-time at my age did have implications. It indicated that I was not going to progress any further up my particular career ladder and that not only would I not gain more status, I would lose some. For me this has probably been the most difficult aspect of moving to part-time work. But negative thoughts about the loss of status can be combated by thinking about the flexibility and freedom I now have and by taking satisfaction from combining a happy family life and a satisfying career.

Another way in which I had to deal with the negatives was the realisation that the whole process would need conscious management otherwise I could end up with too much to do in my part-time role. Also aspects of my work were totally enjoyable and I was not prepared to give them up, but at the same time I wanted to cut out the work that was less rewarding. Finally there were the obvious financial implications of working less to be considered.

### Transitions

Being part of the Retiring Women group gave me an opportunity to express these thoughts and work through these and related issues. The first residential weekend in particular made me realise that it was valid to be a person in transition and that the move into retirement was not going to be the last transition in life that I would make. I realised that, although it was slightly painful to give up on my career, I had actually achieved a great deal, particularly in the last 15 years and that I had made quite a good job of combining career and family life and that I should recognise this and celebrate it. I was able to realise that a change at 60+ to a different way of working could be positive. I recorded in my notes of the first Retiring Women weekend away that 'I felt a split second of excitement', rather than the despondency and even fear that the thought of retirement had previously engendered.

To start with, the move to part-time work felt very strange. During the development of my career, work had come to dominate my life. Although I did always try and take off at least one whole day in the week (usually Saturday), work was never far from my mind. I would actually sneak off to my study to work, pretending that I was doing other things. With this mindset it was initially very odd to be working for less than half of the week.

One of the potential problems with part-time work is feeling excluded and overlooked when at work. This can be a serious issue particularly for part-timers on a permanent contract. I think that I was fortunate that so many people do work part-time at the Institute where the culture seems to be inclusive of them. Part-timers serve on committees, take part in professional development and seem to be offered the same opportunities as full-timers. Obviously there are opportunities and meetings that will be missed in a shorter than normal week, and there are organisations that are not as tolerant of or as dependent on part-timers where they may be treated less well.

Part-time work as a transition into retirement offers the opportunity to start to develop the dormant interests and hobbies that will be important in later years. A demanding full-time job does not leave many opportunities for doing this and part-time work allows the time to explore all the options about where and how you will live and to prioritise what you would like to do.

### Being realistic about part-time commitment

The usual reaction I had from people when they heard I was moving from full-time to part-time work was doubt that I would really reduce the workload and would continue to work just as hard but for less money. I was prepared for the change by a conversation I had with someone who had cut back from full-time to three days a week a few years earlier. When I asked her how things were going, she replied, with only the slightest irony, that the difference was that: 'now I don't work at the week-ends'. I was determined that that would not happen to me and that I was going to try and stick more or less to the three days a week. As a Yorkshire woman the thought of working for five days and being paid for three went against the grain! I therefore prepared for the change by arranging to resign from one of my responsibilities. I realised that I would not have been able to fit my work into three days without making a meaning-ful cut in the work I had to do. I can't pretend that I did not occasionally slip into working occasionally on my days off, but I did mostly succeed. Initially, the way that I found to protect myself from working when I shouldn't was to stick to working the same three days a week – in my case, Tuesday, Wednesday and Thursday, and to organise something definite for Monday and Friday. It might be a trip out with a friend, or even an entry in the diary telling me that this was a day when I was going to clear out my office at home. I found, and still find, that an entry in my diary works like magic for me, telling me what I am supposed to do. It took about six months before I felt natural with the three days a week. It was an enormous change to stop working full-time as it meant that my work no longer takes priority in my life. The reduction from three days a week was a much less traumatic change than the initial decision to scale down.

### Enjoying the work

Being part-time means that it is possible to be proactive and ensure that your workload is focused on the things that you want to do. My current workload focuses on my specific research interests and virtually nothing else. It is great to be able to do this after a number of years when an administrative load took up a large part of my working life and my research interests seemed to get squeezed out.

There is obviously a difference between working part-time on a permanent contract and working part-time after retirement. If you are on a permanent contract, there will be a greater obligation to be a good organisational 'citizen' attending meetings, although sticking to the same days for work each week means that it is clear that you cannot automatically attend meetings on your non-working days. Working part-time after retirement means that it becomes a matter of your choice in most cases whether you attend any meetings at all, although this does mean that you are no longer fully in the picture with regard to changes in the organisation, and are likely to feel gradually less involved.

### Finance

Part-time work means part-time rates of pay. For me moving to part-time work at the same age as I qualified for a State pension lessened the loss of earnings, particularly as once officially a pensioner there is no need to pay National Insurance contributions. Benefits in terms of free travel for Londoners or reduced travel on the national rail services help the finances. My generation of women is almost the last to get the State pension at 60. From April 2010 the State pension age for women starts to increase to 65 and the intention is that by 2046 the pension age for all will be 68.

Formal retirement means starting to receive personal pension payments. Obviously the size of payments depends on the number of years you have worked, and the level of pay for the last few years of work. Continuing to work, whether on a short-term contract or via consultancy, tops up the pension and then there may be other payments like royalties on top of that. Certainly the impact of loss of earnings is softened by not only pension payments but also the reduction in the day-to-day expenses of going to work. The net reduction may be smaller than anticipated.

### Summing up – part-time work as a way into retirement

Going part-time softens the impact of retirement in lots of ways. It provides you with the possibility of choosing what you want to concentrate on for the remainder of your working life, and gives you time to begin to develop the other interests that will be vital to you once you have finally retired. It gives you space to think about priorities and longer term plans, for example the possibility of moving to a new location, or more leisurely and different types of travel for enjoyment. It may also provide a useful financial cushion, topping up your pension. However, there are things that you have to come to terms with. In particular you will probably be signalling that you are reaching the end of your working life and therefore your work-related status will, at best, remain the same and will probably start to decrease.

Unless the Finnish approach of allowing older workers more flexibility is adopted here, the possibility of part-time work is the only realistic option that provides those approaching retirement age with a cushion of time that can help with staying fit and healthy. However, it is easy to end up working a full-time or nearly full-time week but being paid a part-time salary. Moving from a really busy and demanding full-time role to a part-time one necessitates careful planning and the ability to say 'no' to things that are not really central to the role agreed. Be sure to give up at least one major area of responsibility. One trick that will help with this is the use of your diary. Make sure that the 'free' days are really kept that way by initially blocking them out with a definite activity, ideally involving someone else, so that you are more likely to stick to your non-work plan.

All in all, take advantage of the transition phase of part-time work to be proactive and to manage the process of moving seamlessly into retirement, scaling down work and scaling up all those other hobbies, activities and plans that you could never find the time for before. If you are worried about the financial implications then take expert advice and do some sums, taking into account not only the income you will be losing but also the work-related expenditure you will no longer have.

## References

Department of Work and Pensions (DWP) (2008) *Research published on how retirement feels,* 8 April, London, Departmental Press Release.

Hirsch, D. (2003) *Crossroads after 50*. York: Joseph Rowntree Foundation; www.jrf.org.uk (accessed April 2008).

Powell, G. and Graves, L. (2003) *Women and Men in Management,* third edition. Thousand Oaks, CA: Sage Publications.

Women and Work Commission (2006) *Shaping a Fairer Future*. London: DTI.

# Chapter 8

# Busy doing nothing…

## Jennifer Evans

*'The trouble with retirement is that you never get a day off.'*
Abe Lemons

> In this chapter Jennifer describes how retirement has provided her with the opportunity to adopt a slower and less stressful way of life in which she responds to her body's natural rhythms. She is developing skills that she values most, that is those that bring her closer to most of humanity. Among these is the special relationship she has with her grandchildren. She talks about helping them learn to cook and grow food on the allotment. She includes some of their favourite recipes. Jennifer also talks about other interests including swimming, holidays with friends, exercising her brain and being involved in community life.

You've heard it said so many times: 'Now I'm retired, I'm so busy, I don't know how I managed to go to work.' Activities which were once squeezed into the margins of a life centred on the important task of *work*, or even more importantly *career*, now take up hours, days or even weeks. For me, I'm like a kid in a sweetshop – I wake up each day thinking: 'Now, which among the delightful range of activities that present themselves will I choose to do today?' And choice is the thing. If I don't want to do something today (for example, clean the house, which mostly I find quite therapeutic), I can always do it tomorrow. If the sun's shining, I can go for a walk, or dig my allotment.

Man-made, clock-based time, according to Jay Griffiths (1999) in her book *Pip Pip: A sideways look at time,* is a product of industrialisation. It's unnatural, in the sense that it forces us to go against the natural rhythms of our bodies, to be awake when we need to sleep, to be active when we need to rest, and to be constrained by an increasingly globalised and fast existence. For women, she argues, this type of existence is especially difficult and damaging, because women's bodies are (still) attuned to natural cycles, influenced by the moon, and this forcing of ourselves into the rhythms of the masculine, man-made, manufacturing processes of the industrial and even the post-industrial system is not healthy or life-enhancing.

What retirement has offered me is a chance to follow a slower and less stressful path. I'm still busy, but I have some choice over when I'm active and when I can rest. I guess I've always, from my schooldays onwards, hated being locked up in a room having to 'work' when I could be outside 'playing'. But the need for survival dictated that 'work' should rule my life, and lots of my work has been like playing – creative and fun, working in teams and solving puzzles – lucky me! The killer work-wise was always the commuting – three hours a day at least. This had two main disbenefits – one that I couldn't base a social life around work, because I was always conscious that I would have at least an hour and a half journey to get home, and the second that I didn't involve myself in my local community because of the long hours I worked.

Having time has allowed me to take the time to meet friends and also make new ones.

So what do I busy myself with?

## Grandchildren

There are a lot of us around, if you look. That is, grandparents looking after grandchildren. They pick up kids from school, look after them in the holidays and generally enjoy that special relationship that means you can have fun without being ultimately responsible. I'm lucky to have six grandchildren living within about 500 metres of my house. We have a park at the end of the road, and it's a short walk into town, so we have lots of opportunities for play and fun. Their age range is from 15 years to 15 months, so we do a variety of things together, in groups of two or three. We go to the park, we buy 'pick and mix' sweets from Woolworths, we go swimming (or rather they go to swimming lessons, and I swim during that time).

One thing all the grandchildren like to do (apart from the very youngest one) is cook. With my eldest granddaughter, we do quite adventurous vegetarian cooking, that she can take home to supply her family with. We try to use produce from the allotment, to give her some idea about seasonality, and also about what things look like when they're growing. Many children don't realise that vegetables grow in dirt in the ground. A friend of mine (a primary head) told me of a child in her school who wouldn't eat potatoes at his grandmother's house because he saw them covered in dirt, as she had dug them up from her garden. So I think it's important that children see the vegetables while they're still in the ground, and that children get a chance to visit local allotments.

The younger ones like baking cakes and biscuits. They sit on the work top and help to stir mixtures on the stove (hazardous) and break eggs into sponge cake mixtures. Here are some of their favourite recipes:

> **Nana's famous flapjack** (their name not mine):
> Melt 100g of butter with 100g of sugar and 1 tablespoonful of golden syrup. When all the sugar has melted and it looks a bit toffee-like, add 200g of porridge oats. Put in an oblong tin and cook for about 20 minutes at 170 °C. Cut into slices while still warm and leave in the tin to cool.

Obviously, the best bit is licking out the saucepan in which you've mixed the flapjack.

Another favourite, which they like to have if invited for dinner is (Nana's famous) mushroom pasta.

> **Nana's famous mushroom pasta:**
> This involves frying a few cloves of garlic and 3 tablespoons of chopped parsley in a couple of ounces of butter and some oil. Then adding a pound of sliced mushrooms and frying until they're well cooked and no liquid remains. Then add half a pint of double cream and heat through. This goes well with farfalle, which is easier for young ones to eat than tagliatelle, which is more usual with this dish.

I think part of my motivation for taking on quite a substantial childcare role with my grandchildren stems from guilt at having been such a busy working mother when my own children were young. It was a necessity (we needed the money), but my career path meant that I worked long hours and was often away from home. My children survived it, but I'm not sure it was optimal to leave them with childminders (or running wild when they were older). So, I feel I can provide a safe place for my grandchildren, where they can relax and feel at home, as well as enabling my own children to follow their careers without so much worry about what might be happening to their offspring. I also think it's important for children to have relationships with adults of all ages. Like many families, we have a complicated network of stepchildren, half-brothers and sisters, aunts and uncles and in-laws all living nearby, so there are lots of places to go for support and encouragement. My children's (non) nuclear family is not isolated, but very crowded with family, friends and neighbours. It feels very different, both from my own childhood, and from my experience of bringing up children with very little support around. Retirement has given me that opportunity to be involved and useful – two very important antidotes to getting old and depressed.

## The allotment

I've always had a hankering towards self-sufficiency and growing my own fruit and veg. But the combination of a very pressured job and a very small garden meant that this bit of my dream life has had to wait – until now. I acquired my allotment four years ago, before I retired, and to be honest, it's been hard work to keep it under control. This year has been the first time I've felt that I've been on the winning team against weeds, bugs, birds and the weather. I'm not going to be self-sufficient, but currently have two sacks of potatoes in the shed, along with a good supply of onions and garlic, as well as lots of lettuces, beans and other greens in the ground. I've just finished reading Barbara Kingsolver's (2007) book *Animal, Vegetable, Miracle* in which she describes her family's year of living more or less completely from what they could grow and rear on their small farm. The book is part polemic against industrial farming methods and the appalling diet foisted on Americans, and the environmental and health consequences that brings, and part celebration of the trials and triumphs of self-sufficiency.

Keeping an allotment is a subversive activity and I see it as one small way of resisting the control of my life by big corporations. I try to shop at farmers' markets for meat and cheese, and also try to buy locally where I can. I felt a huge rapport with Barbara Kingsolver's ideas and aims, although I don't think I will ever be as dedicated as she is. Apparently she's been nominated the seventy-fourth most dangerous person in the USA for trying to undermine the corporate food business. I like the idea of being dangerous.

One of my partner's colleagues at the Citizens Advice Bureau, where he works as a volunteer, said, when he was describing a lovely meal we'd had from the allotment produce: 'Well isn't it easier to just go to the supermarket?' Well, if you like really fresh food, grown organically and almost free (apart from the cost of the seeds), it's not easier to go to the supermarket. Neither is it easier on the environment to transport food for hundreds or thousands of miles, and spray it with chemicals when it's growing, or degrade the land by using chemical fertilisers. It's quicker, of course, but I'm all in favour of the Slow Movement (www.slowfood.com), which encourages us to be more in tune with our own rhythms and those of our locality.

There are other benefits to having an allotment too. For one, you're outside in the fresh air, in a lovely environment (even if you live in a town or city), surrounded by greenery and bird song. You're getting physical exercise, which is purposeful (I can't see the point of running or aerobics, and although I swim, I find it very boring). Another benefit is the chance to meet people that you wouldn't normally come across – mainly old men, with a wealth of knowledge about growing vegetables in your particular environment. They're also very generous and will share produce and plants. In my first year at the allotment, my neighbour Pete gave me three rhubarb crowns, which have given pounds and pounds of fruit each year. He also gave me Jerusalem artichokes, which spread like nobody's business and make a wonderful soup.

Growing your own and eating seasonally has brought about a profound change in the way I approach meal planning and cooking. Instead of thinking: 'What would I like to cook today?', and then going out to buy the ingredients, I look at what I've got in the allotment, or from the farmers' market and then think: 'What can I make with this?' Tonight we had one of the many meals that use up gluts of courgettes – boureki. The recipe I follow comes from a small book written by an English woman (Cradick 2006) who fell in love and married a Cretan guy and opened a small taverna in his village, overlooking Souda Bay. Elizabeth and her friend from university days also started a small travel company that encouraged local families to renovate old stone Cretan houses and let them out to visitors. The company – Pure Crete – organises flights and lets the accommodation. We've stayed in the village many times over the last ten years or so, and have seen two more tavernas and a small grocery shop open, but essentially the place stays the same. Here's Elizabeth's boureki recipe, which she got from a friend in the village:

---

**Elizabeth's boureki:**
Thinly slice about 600g courgettes and 600g potatoes. Mix in a bowl with a tub of ricotta (in place of the Greek cheese which you can't easily get in the UK), a tablespoon of fresh chopped mint, one or two cloves of garlic and a tablespoon of olive oil and salt and pepper. Bake at 170 °C for 45 minutes. Then grate over 100g of hard cheese (I use cheddar, Elizabeth suggests Edam) and pour over this one egg beaten with a little milk. Put it back in the oven for a further 20 minutes. And there you are – delicious, cheap and simple to make.

---

Another good way to use up courgettes is to fry them gently (as many as you like, but a half a kilo would be good for two people), with lots of chopped garlic, until the courgettes are quite mushy. Then stir in a couple of tablespoonfuls of cream and lots of grated parmesan cheese and black pepper. Serve with pasta.

## Exercise

I'm not great with exercise and don't spend a lot of time on it, although I know it's important to keep active and mobile as you get older. I try to walk everywhere, as far as I can, and it's more possible now, because the pressures on time are less. We also go on several walking holidays a year, and for long walks at home when there's a holiday looming in order to get fit. The walking holidays are those where you walk from hotel to hotel and someone takes your luggage. We tend to choose ones that aren't too demanding (no dizzy heights or scrambling), but good long walks of between 10 and 12 miles each day.

I also swim twice a week, when I take two of my grandchildren to their swimming lessons. I used to sit and watch them, and then decided it was more fun to swim. After the lessons we have a game of 'Crocodile', which is essentially tag in the water. Unfortunately for me they are much faster swimmers so I get caught a lot. I also spend a lot of time laughing, so that slows me up quite a bit. I read in *The Guardian* today that swimming is the ideal exercise for those aged between 60 and 70, and I must say there are quite a few older people in the pool when I'm there.

## Holidays

A friend has remarked that I'm 'good at holidays'. I think she means finding interesting places to go, and then going to them. I found it a necessity when working, to get away and have a break, even if I often ended up taking work with me. Now I've retired, I'm not planning to cut down much, but maybe take slightly different holidays to reduce my use of aeroplanes. I like going to simple rural places, and walking, so my ideal holiday is to spend time in beautiful countryside in Italy, France, Greece or Turkey, walking, exploring and eating local food. Getting to these places by train and bus may take a little longer, but since time is not so pressing, it may be possible to do.

## Exercising the brain

I have a dream that one day I will live in France. Until then, I'm preparing myself by taking up French again after 44 years, and doing a diploma with the Open University. I've just spent a week at the University of Caen, on the summer school attached to the course. I've found the course very stimulating and interesting, but also very time-consuming. I don't really give it enough time, but I also don't feel under pressure to get top marks. As long as I get a good enough mark not to get thrown off the course, I'll be satisfied. When I met other participants at the summer school I realised that the course was much more of a pressure for them, as they mainly were struggling to manage work and family commitments, as well as studying for a degree. I feel fortunate that, for me, the course is a source of pleasure and not of stress. That's one of the benefits of being retired, I guess. The course materials themselves are excellent and the topics covered have kept me interested and involved. They included politics, environmental issues, culture and the arts, gender equality and health.

Another of my brain-exercising activities is to attempt *The Guardian* crossword every day. It's not often finished, and I squeeze it in during lunch and coffee breaks. I have a fellow crossword doer, who texts me now and then to compare progress. I've heard that these kinds of lateral thinking and code-breaking activities help to ward off Alzheimer's – I hope that's so, as I'm noticing more and more brain lapses as I just can't call to mind that word I know perfectly well, or I get to the top of the stairs and forget what I've come for.

I'm also still doing a small amount of research and report writing, as part of a project team carrying out an evaluation of an initiative to fast-track suitable candidates into headship. I'm hoping to carry on with small pieces of work like this into the foreseeable future, as long as they don't take up too much of my precious time. I find doing the interviews and analysing and reporting data enjoyable, as I know I'm doing something I'm good at, and experienced at. I can work from home and I can also enjoy the chance to be part of a team and to be valued for my contribution. (The money's useful, too.)

## Community involvement

As I mentioned in the introduction, for most of my career, I commuted daily into London, which left very little time for being involved in my own community. I'm currently a school governor – a grandparent governor, as my eldest granddaughter is at the school, and two more grandchildren are lined up to go there over the next few years. It's been interesting to be a governor in a school which faces none of the inner-city problems confronting most of the schools I've had contact with through my work. I've noticed a complacency and a lack of drive in the school, compared with many of the London schools I'm familiar with. I would say that the school is 'coasting' although its latest Ofsted report described it as 'good'. However, it's interesting to be involved in the life of a school, in its exam results, its fund-raising activities and its sporting and cultural achievements. Having time to visit the school during the day is also useful and keeps me in touch with developments.

## Time for friends

One of my greatest pleasures is to meet up with friends to go to a gallery or a film, or go for a walk – or even shopping, though it's not my favourite activity. The Retiring Women group is a great source of support and inspiration – the women in the group are so creative and independent-minded and have all approached retirement in different and admirable ways. They do voluntary work, they paint, they sing, they write, they knit, they garden, they go to exhibitions, they read books and see films that they can share, they acquire dogs and occasionally grandchildren. What's not to love?

A regret is that, although I now have time, I cannot spend it with my mother, as she died earlier this year. I would have liked more time to talk and to look after her, as she became very frail in the last year of her life, but even though I was retired, I found it difficult to make the 240-mile round trip to Dorset more than once a week. I miss her profoundly, and I think that many of the things I now do – the jam-making, gardening, vegetable growing and the cooking are a sort of homage to her and her way of life, which was so different from mine.

I've come to realise, although I think I always knew it, that I value most highly those skills that bring us closer to most of humanity: of growing and preparing food, looking after children, nurturing our families and living well in our communities. This is not to devalue a professional life spent in education or to regret that I didn't take another route through life. It's more to put that phase of my life into perspective and to look forward to a new phase which links more closely to my personal and emotional history as well as directing me to a different future.

## References

Griffiths, Jay (1999) *Pip Pip: A sideways look at time*. London: Flamingo.
Kingsolver, B., with Camille Kingsolver and Steven L. Hopp (2007) *Animal, Vegetable, Miracle, our year of seasonal eating*. London: Faber & Faber. Also http://www.animalvegetablemiracle.com/
Cradick, Elizabeth (2006) *Cretan Village Cooking: Traditional recipes from the taverna* Τα Ατερα.

# Chapter 9

# Reflections on gender and retiring

## Anne Gold

'*When men reach their sixties and retire, they go to pieces. Women go right on cooking.*'

Gail Sheehy

> This interview focuses on Anne's special interest in gender. She examines the academic work she has been involved in and relates her learning to the processes of retiring. This is a personal reflection in which Anne talks about how she has come to terms with retiring, a very new experience, and how gender issues relate to the way she thinks about recent transitions. Anne looks in particular at the changes she has seen during her working life in relation to employment and domestic roles and how she detects differences in the ways her children and their partners are approaching things.

Anne Gold: I have now been retired two and a half months, and four weeks of that I have been on holiday so I can't really tell you much about being retired, but I can tell you what my life was like before.

*Interviewer: What experiences have you had in your working life and what have you learned about gender and work?*

I have been involved in education and teaching for 43 years and I always thought that life was unfair for women but for many years that felt like a personal crusade, rather than a wide field of academic and social discourse.

I taught for ten years in a mixed school and then I worked in a girls' school. I was able to read the micro-politics of the two sorts of school I worked in, after a year or so in each school. There were enormous differences between them, due, I'm sure, to the differently gendered ethos of the two schools. The effects of gender could be seen in the ways the schools were organised, both officially and unofficially.

Then I moved to the Institute of Education. In moving from a school where I had taught for ten years and which I left as a very senior teacher to an initially unfathomable, huge-seeming place of higher education, I couldn't read the organisation for two or three years. Actually it was only when I joined the Centre for Research in Gender and Education (CREG) that I began to understand it. That is because my own academic field of leadership and management gave me a formal understanding of organisations, and CREG helped me to read the gender dimensions.

I began as a lecturer in a Management Unit. I was appointed to run short courses for people who were interested in School Leadership. At that time – the late 1980s and early 1990s – the London Boroughs were having trouble recruiting enough women for headship. So I began to think about women and leadership in schools, and about being a woman working in higher education (HE).

I was concerned at that point both about bringing more women into educational leadership and understanding what it felt like for me as a woman working in an organisation which was very gendered. My experience, and that of many other women, found the higher education context to be patriarchal for those teaching and learning in it. And even though school teaching is 'women's work', one would expect that this place of higher education would employ and promote more women than usual in HE. But it continues to be gendered. Men are more likely to be promoted and they seem to know automatically what they have to do to get promoted. They know, as if by osmosis, how promotions are done. And even after promotion, women professors earn less than men. In HE in general, the research that women tend to want to do is not recognised as worthwhile and 'good' – all of those things have enormous gender dimensions.

It's interesting now on retirement, that I find myself doing things which I never really had time for and which I thought were less important than work. Although I had two children and I worked full-time for most of their childhoods I never really, as a mother, just relaxed when having young babies around because I had my work and I also had to manage the house and the home. Now I get tremendous joy out of just watching my grandchildren develop communication and that's not about being a grandmother that's about having time to watch.

I wish I had been more relaxed earlier in my life but I think one of the things about working women is that they are never just working women. Most women of my generation, however helpful and supportive their partners are, were the primary carers: for their children and often for their own parents and even if they didn't cook every day, they were the ones who had to make sure there was enough food and that the washing was done and the house was clean. Even if you had help from your partner to do it you were the one that was primarily responsible.

So, as a working woman working life was never just focusing on work. There were all sorts of other strands and responsibilities going on at the same time. Now, having stopped paid work, the other strands and responsibilities are still there, apart from bringing up children. But one of the things I have noticed is that I don't have to say 'I wish I had time to deal with that' so, for example, I found myself yesterday making sure the taps shone which I have never done before because I like the taps shining and I had time to do it.

The work I did at the Institute brought with it quite a lot of respect internally and externally so micro-politically, I think I was quite high profile. I talk a lot so I made myself quite high profile. So on retirement, I have gone from having a job that was quite high profile to being mainly at home and coming to terms with not being high profile. And partly I love that and partly I am talking myself through it and saying 'A girl doesn't have to be high profile – you just have to be useful.' It is interesting living with a partner who was also high profile professionally, and who is also not so much anymore. We talk about this quite a lot together. We have both had international recognition and then to be at home and not in paid work so much now does contrast with that time towards the end of our working lives when we were both high status.

I think for me it is easier in a way because I go off and look after my grandchildren and still see students and I am happy to go for long walks. I think I am quite careful in thinking about what it means to me to have been high status and to ask myself whether I really need it. My partner is also very well aware of these issues but doesn't have all the other bits in his life. He has never had to take main responsibility for the house, the home and the cooking, although he has now started cooking. So in a way he has never had the opportunities I have had to dissipate that focus. I think probably, women have many focuses and men don't.

I don't think that is so true of the next generation. My son and son-in-law are much more involved in the home and have a focus on their children to the extent that one of them was the main carer for two years and one of them has reduced his work to four days a week in order to be with his daughter. So my observations around gender are that for my generation of women retiring and men retiring, things are different to people in their thirties and it is changing a lot.

*So when you said you think it is easier for you, was that about being easier for you than your partner in terms of the retiring process because you have had all of those different responsibilities throughout your life?*

I do think that a lot of men I know do have a lot of responsibilities now they are retired. It is just that it's because they have had one main focus before retirement. When their paid work stopped they have either developed other focuses or they have been quite lost. They have to develop other interests on retirement, whereas women of my generation still do all the other stuff as well. So I am not sitting at home doing nothing. I am still shopping and washing and cooking and making sure the family is OK but I have more time to do it. And I can take my time over these things and they can come to the forefront of what I do now, whereas before they had to fit in with my working life. I often felt torn about all the things I had to do but now it's less hurried. But I am only a few months into the process of retiring!

*You mentioned before that you thought you might have gone through a period of adjustment already?*

I have seen people retire, and my father was one of them, who get depressed because suddenly they feel empty, and I am quite prone to melancholy. I remember when I was offered a place to do an MA full-time in my mid-forties. I put it off for a year because I was worried I would crumble – there wouldn't be a me in the middle of it. I probably felt that stopping work would mean that I would be thrown on to myself and I would have no paid work structure to support my construct of myself, so I would find that I was empty or whatever. I found myself worrying about this for a long time again when I came near to retirement. I remember my father had chest pains for a year before he retired. I think he had the very same sort of worry that he never articulated. He just didn't want to retire. So I spent a lot of time being worried about retiring before it happened – perhaps for eight years, but most intensely for about six months before. You know, I had decided to retire at 60 (when I was still young enough to begin new ventures) and then I sort of forgot and went on to 64 (laughs) partly because the work I was doing became more and more interesting.

But the minute I retired we went to Peru for three weeks and I think I am still not fitting everything I want to do into my life. So it isn't empty and frightening!

*So it is not turning out as badly as you were anticipating?*

Not so far. I don't know what it is going to feel like when I have got through all my projects although I might then develop new ones.

Another thing is that I am very lucky that I can afford to retire, and I don't have to worry about money. If I want to go to an art gallery or cinema I can afford to go. I don't think I would feel as good if I couldn't afford entertainment or access things to look at and do. Being in London and having free transport is all part of that.

*So what do you think helped you in that period coming up to retiring?*

Well perhaps I am manic: I found myself walking in the pouring rain yesterday singing at the top of my voice which I think is manic, not just ordinary (laughs). So you see I probably am still worried.

I think the Retiring Women group helped me for the last three years by providing a space dedicated to thinking about these issues and to hearing other people planning and talking. I think if I hadn't thought about retirement, if I hadn't reflected on it and tried to make sense of it before, it would have hit me quite painfully. But I think that having a dedicated space where I could hear other people's stories was important. Also our time together allowed me to realise that there were a couple of things that I wanted to do on retirement, and that I have done – that realisation came through thinking and talking in the group.

*Do you want to say what those things are?*

Yes, one is that I have done and still wanted to do something voluntary within the community and now I have more time. I was reminded of this and I registered with Reach and I am going to see people this week to talk about starting something (www.reach-online.org.uk). That will give me a sense of purpose, of doing something worthwhile.

The other thing is that the group has given me permission not to do anything some days, so I can sit and read – just to go slower. I have stopped telling myself off about wasting time. And the things I did before that I considered wasting time are not wasting time – like reading my novel in the daytime, or watching a serial I missed all afternoon, which I would never have done before. I think I am in the process of redefining what being useful is. And I do have a partner so I am never lonely. Sometimes we go to art galleries together and sometimes I go by myself, or I walk. I have noticed though that we both still need our own space. It's quite important that we have our own working rooms – we have each taken one of our children's bedrooms as our work rooms.

*And do you go in that room everyday?*

Not when we were sharing a laptop! Can you believe we managed to do that when mine broke? I think he was amazing because it is quite important for both of us to get online regularly, but we managed it for several weeks. Now I have just got mine mended. The door isn't shut in either of the rooms and we shout to each other. We sometimes can't hear each other so we accuse each other of developing deafness (laughs).

*I wonder if you want to say any more about how you see men and women retiring differently?*

I suppose it is something about filling days: I could fill my day cleaning, washing, shopping, cooking and ironing and I suppose women still have the house and family to fall back on. I don't think men have quite those fillers. Although they may cook it is still usually cooking only when they want to, not the regular supporting our lives sort of cooking. But again that's our generation. I don't see that in my children's generation. I see them taking equal parts. It will be very interesting to see what happens when they retire.

*You said that your partner does some cooking, so do you think in the future things will even out even more in how people approach retiring?*

It is not regular the way he cooks and we both make a fuss about it. So it doesn't feel like it is part of the daily ongoing supporting our lives type of thing although it is a great pleasure having him do the cooking. Since he retired he is taking much more interest in the household generally – he has been making appointments for people to come and do work in the house and he has been hanging around for them. There was a year when I was still working and he had retired and it wasn't like that awful, carefully balanced house of cards any more: he was at home seeing to things. That was a lot better, so maybe that is part of the relaxedness too – that he is at home most of the time.

*And did he prepare in the way you did for retiring?*

No, I don't think so. In fact he still edits two journals and does a bit of teaching, so he doesn't have a day when there isn't something that he needs to be doing for work but that is the way he has chosen to fill his life.

*And for both of you will that element of work continue?*

I've got to the stage when I think I don't want to teach any more or support students, although I love these, after next year. I'd like to see how the voluntary work thing goes, to improve my French, to be regularly involved with our grandchildren. I'd like to write, maybe, but not academically, to go to a show every week, to a film every week. There is so much to do in London that I am still not getting round to. I have never found teaching easy: I feel it is a bit of a performance and I get stage fright beforehand and I can never sleep before a new piece of teaching. It's almost a superstition, it takes a lot out of me but the more you give the more you get back. I know I do it well, but I think about the energy and tension involved.

I still have to do seven lectures in Singapore next February, two days' teaching in Iceland and a week's teaching here in March and I am already worrying about all that. I don't think I want that fear anymore and it would be quite good for me to stop, although I love teaching and it defines me. Part of me thinks that one shouldn't be doing things one knows how to do and doing them just to feel good. Maybe I need to do more emotional searching.

*Can I go back to something you said earlier about being useful, do you think that's a gendered thing?*

I don't think it is actually. I know a lot of men who are doing voluntary work outside the home but I don't know whether that is about being useful or whether that is about status. I think it is upbringing, culture, it comes out of people's spiritual understanding, people's relationship with the world around them. So it's very complicated.

*I was wondering if anything in your work life has connected with what you are thinking about in retiring? What have you got out of your work life that is helping you now?*

I am finally developing a respect for my own intellect which has taken me 40 years to develop. I don't have to prove it anymore because I know it is there. I've also learnt to be reflective and to connect what is going on with other spaces as well as the reading so maybe what I have got out of my work life is how to think. I don't know whether that has or hasn't helped me now and I think it probably has as here I am thinking. It is very noisy in my head and I think that's probably doing a lot of thinking which is what my work entailed.

I have got confidence out of my work life, but that's not gendered…. Yes it is! I think women and girls of my generation were brought up without self-confidence and I think we were brought up to think that having confidence meant that you were a show-off. I am from the North West of England and I think that that was in the 1950s (during my formative years) a Methodist, Puritanical part of the country. To be different or to show off were the two worst sins. So I was part of a family of immigrants – we were different and as a child of intellectuals we were different. I spent a lot of my childhood apologising for myself, and quite a lot of my early adulthood feeling out of place. Probably through my work life, my final work life in higher education (although I have found a lot of it very painful, because I always thought I wasn't intellectually good enough) I finally came to a place where I didn't have to apologise to myself anymore or apologise for what I thought or the way I thought it. This is because I have spent a long time thinking and writing about power: about how to empower others, and what it felt like to be disempowered, which I think is based on such issues as gender, race and class. And I'd lived it myself, but I hadn't articulated it. I think that now I have articulated it and had it heard, written it in books, had it valued, I think I am probably in a much better place intellectually than I ever was before. Because I am now an older woman it is accepted that I feel what I feel and think what I think because I have been given permission through my working life to do that. I think that may be gendered.

*It strikes me that you are emotional, talking about that?*

No, it made me feel proud. Oh – that's a sin! (laughs). I think it might make me feel emotional if I wasn't trying to articulate it so carefully. If I wasn't concerned with articulation I might have a quick cry.

That was a good question because I have never really connected the two. I knew intellectually that retiring should be moving on, not ending, but this has made me think about what personal growing I am taking with me.

*Yes, there is something I have got from editing the book and that is about the way in which people have led their working lives and how they are leading their retiring lives. The sorts of things people are connecting from their work lives and learning about in retiring. I think you have articulated that sense of connection really well.*

Yes, well, I suppose the other bit for me is the international dimension. I live with a Hungarian and between us, our parents came from different parts of Europe.

I live an international life, so I think for me it has been the other way round. I did international work because I am international rather than became international through my work.

I live an international life. When I was a child in the North West of England, shortly after the last world war, I had to hide the international dimension of my life and be ashamed of it because I lived in a small town and it was hard to be different, as I said before. And that is the main reason I came to London and stayed in London because it is a big, international, bustling city where I could hide, and I grew up in a small town where I just couldn't fit. So the whole international thing about my family: one child lives in France, my daughter is married to a man whose family come from Sri Lanka – all of that is my life anyway and it fed my work and it doesn't matter that I'm retired. It has made me think not about what work has done to our lives but what our life has offered our work and you can sometimes only see that afterwards.

*Thank you very much. Is there anything that you would like to add?*

Well you asked me about the gender dimension and I'd like to say that the Retiring Women group was very important to me because it was all women and that is about the way I function: I was brought up to do emotional house-work with men, to look after them and help them feel comfortable. But when I am in a group where I am looking at my feelings, and at things that have helped and hindered me, oppressed me and empowered me, because my life and our lives are so gendered, I need freedom to feel and think. I know it was important for me personally to be in a group with just women because it feels freer talking about issues that are not overtly gendered but I would not have wanted to talk in front of men about. Maybe I would have wanted to protect men. So I still believe we still need women-only spaces if only to help us deal better with the gendered life.

*Thank you. I really wanted your voice to be in the book.*

I find it quite hard now to understand why I couldn't write my story myself for the book. Perhaps I couldn't write about retirement because I hadn't done it but it loomed ahead of me. And I didn't know what else to write about and I know I had some anger or discomfort about how difficult it was for me to find something authentic to write about. I know I have sounded quite obstreperous about not wanting to write, like a denial of something. I think that was connected with the six months leading up to retiring when I was probably doing all that emotional work. That was probably anger about ending, finishing, worrying about how to do it properly and anxiety about how to do it properly. So in much the same way that I feel far more relaxed now than I ever dreamt I would be and having a far better time than I felt I would, probably if you asked me in three months' time to write I'd love to, but that's too late (laughs). So thank you for asking me to do this.

*Thank you.*

# Chapter 10

# Even busier in my Third Age

## Ashley Kent

*'Retirement at sixty-five is ridiculous. When I was sixty-five I still had pimples.'*

George Burns

> In this chapter Ashley reflects on some personal experiences that influenced his decisions about retiring. He recounts how he planned for his retirement, arranging for a smooth takeover of his work with his successors and his retirement party and took financial advice. Still actively involved in many activities, Ashley proves a very positive example of an important transition.

How did I decide to retire? Well, it crept up on me really and in the last few years before retirement I began to think increasingly about it. Until then it was very much on the back burner but as I began to think about it I became keener and more ready. I suppose it was the experience of three close family members that was pivotal in my decision. Probably most significant was the totally unexpected sudden death of my wife Katherine prematurely, aged 53, seven years ago. She was a vibrant, lively, apparently well woman who died from a deep vein thrombosis. That shocking experience suggested to me very forcibly that one does not know what is round the corner and one 'should live each day as if thy last'. I hope for a long, varied and exciting retirement which Kate never had. The second influence was that of Pappy (my father-in-law) who died within a year of retiring from a lengthy career in the Civil Service. Building up to his retirement he and Nanny (my mother-in-law) spent over ten years rebuilding a derelict country house in Provence with the intention of spending more time there on retirement. That was never to be. The third and rather different influence was that of my father who retired from active work as a business man at 50 and spent the rest of his life – he died at 90 or so

– travelling, working part-time and having a varied and fulfilled last 40 years! I aspire to be like my father and not like my wife and father-in-law.

The other powerful feeling was that I had enjoyed a most fortunate, success-ful and happy career, reaching positions I had never dreamt of. I never expected to be a professor and head of geography at the Institute of Education in the University of London; president of the Geographical Association; chairman of the Council of British Geography; executive member of the International Geographical Union and chair of the International Geographical Union British Committee; author of a number of books and other publications – and so it goes on. As well as these activities I enjoyed most of them and so was doubly fortunate.

I began to have the feeling that I had 'done it before' – the publications, organising and attending conferences, leading and innovating new curricula and the rest. My gut feeling was that my enthusiasm for all this life was begin-ning to wane and I had new, different aspirations.

At the same time a new and vibrant geography team was emerging at the Institute and I felt more than confident they could be successful 'guardians' of the Institute's 'Geography Heritage' about which I care passionately. I felt I could 'hand over' with confidence to a new generation. This confidence was reinforced when two former colleagues were appointed on a job share to take up my position. The 'shop' couldn't have been left in better hands!

At the same time I began to realise that approaching the maximum service term (40 years) I was in a financially strong position to retire. I also reminded myself that I had always had a range of interests and friends beyond my work and that expanding those would be enjoyable and feasible. I had never lived to work – I had always had a full 'other' life that consisted of family, friends, travel, competitive sport of various types, film, theatre and property.

Being a practical chap I spent most time in the early days of considering retirement on whether it was financially feasible and if so what financial deci-sions to take. I had frankly taken very little interest or notice in these matters and was naive about them in the extreme. I began to read the relevant sections in the newspapers, sent off for appropriate booklets and in particular spoke to two university friends who had retired recently. I sought, in the first instance, professional advice from three financial advisers. One had been a person who had successfully advised colleagues at the Institute for many years and in the past had given me sound advice. I met up with him once at my place of work. Another I met through a retirement course organised by the university and paid for by my institution. He had presented the financial element of the day's course and offered a personal consultation. I met with him face to face twice, both times in my home. He started me off with helpful paperwork and intro-duced the broad options open to me. The third adviser to whom I ultimately gave my business was a friend and colleague of my accountant who I entirely trust. The possibility of a 'seamless web' between accountant and financial adviser appealed a great deal. I met this man twice in my mother's home in northern England and liked his straightforward and clear explanations.

What was clear from these three advisers was that their advice was broadly similar – an encouraging sign! In my case I opted for a lower pension with a maximum lump sum that included additional voluntary contributions (AVCs), which I had accumulated over the years. The lump sum was invested in an OEIC (open ended investment company – historically known as unit trusts) known as a 'tax wrapper'.

A key moment in the period leading up to retirement was attending a retirement course laid on by the University of London and paid for by the Institute of Education. It proved to be a well-organised, useful and enjoyable day. About 20 people attended (all approaching retirement) and there were some interesting whole-group and small-group discussions. Sharing of experience permeated the day and the overall feeling I left with was that I was not unlike many people at the same stage of life and that I was ahead of many in my thinking about and preparing for retirement. The organisers, recent retirees who had set up a business running such courses, provided full documentation incorporating a lot of useful contact addresses and possibilities.

Having made the decision to retire I consulted with my head of academic group and arranged an early meeting with the director of the Institute, Geoff Whitty. Although I had expressed the wish to retire completely in the summer of 2007 I was content to continue until the end of 2007 so as to be counted as a 'research active' member of staff for the important activity in which the Institute's research activities were to be judged (the Research Assessment Exercise). What I was sure of was that I wanted to retire completely and not phase in retirement which some colleagues prefer.

Having spoken to the director I immediately informed my geography colleagues of my intentions and had some role in encouraging possible successors to apply for my position. Most important, it seems to me, was discussing with geography colleagues when and how to pass over responsibilities. This was then firmed up with my eventual successors once they were appointed. I was keen to give colleagues as much notice as possible and help ease the transition as far as possible.

What then began to exercise my mind was the retirement function. A little like a wedding or funeral it is an event that can only be held once – and I wanted it to be a happy and positive occasion. I had attended a number of retirement 'dos' and had as a result fairly clear views as to what I wanted. What I did not want was an over formal affair with lengthy speeches and responses. I was keen that all Institute staff be invited through *This Week* (the weekly staff newsletter) and I wanted it to be held late afternoon, no later, so colleagues felt able to stay a little time. Notice needed to be given to possible attendees and I was happy for it to be held in the staff dining room, with a simple buffet. Booking the room and alerting the catering department was a critical early task. So too was discussing the nature of the function with colleagues and in particular with the former colleague who was to be 'chair' of the event. I had also decided that only a limited number of former colleagues and students were to be invited making it very much a celebration with present colleagues. I was particularly keen that non-academic colleagues at the Institute were invited since they were important in my happy time there.

Strangely I became a little anxious about the event. For instance would people come, would it be highly embarrassing? In fact it was, in my eyes, highly successful. A range of colleagues attended and there were some super 'vignettes' of my life presented by colleagues: the director as overview; one colleague as a longstanding friend; another as my first line manager; a PhD student; and my successor – the master of ceremonies. I then tried to respond both briefly and lightly.

I enjoyed the whole thing and was able to share it with my immediate family – an important aspect I feel. There was a good turnout, I received a most useful and appropriate gift and I was left having a warm feeling about the event. I was most touched by the heartfelt messages sent to me by those who were unable to attend. Overall (as I know full well as a teacher) the careful planning paid off!

My broad approach from the start has been to withdraw from most work commitments and responsibilities whether within the Institute or beyond. I really wanted to have a clean break and begin the next phase of my life. So from the summer of 2008 I resigned from the Executive Committee of the International Geographical Union (IGU) and its related British Committee. I also deliberately did not attend the UK's Geographical Association annual conference and the equivalent of the IGU's Olympics the IGU Congress in Tunisia in 2008.

At the same time I have unashamedly 'cherry picked' some activities for which I have a particular interest. These include: the National School Geography Textbook Collection; chairing the Geographical Association's International Initiatives Fund; co-supervising five PhD students; and some external and PhD examining. I also have some favourite research topics I intend to continue and write about – the history of geographical education at the Institute of Education, children of geographers and memories of place. Related to this ongoing activity I decided to apply formally for the conferred title of emeritus professor. This has advantages both for the Institute and for myself. For myself it means that I can use the library, continue with my Institute email address, and have shared use of an emeritus professors' room, and it gives me the opportunity to respond to future consultancies and research projects.

Well, as I write this I have been retired for six months and, as they say, the time has flown. The majority of my time has been spent on activities that I planned ahead of retirement. So, for instance, I have spent some time refurbishing a property in Cumbria; put final touches to an apartment purchased in France; played tennis for two teams; engaged in a number of leisure and sporting activities including squash, golf and walking; and travelled a good deal.

Perhaps of greater interest are the unintended, unplanned elements of retirement, most of which have been positive! I have joined a fitness centre and attend it regularly, making me feel appropriately well. I organise considerably more visits to the theatre, cinema and concerts than I ever expected. My weekly French classes have proved useful and fun. I have begun successfully to tackle the enjoyable exercise of re-establishing contact with longstanding friends and at the same time begun to make new friends in a home area new to myself but not my partner. I go to quite unexpected and high quality poetry and play readings held at my local library and have acquired a free cricket pass for Middlesex home games – yet to be made use of!

On the negative and unexpected side I have experienced some ankle and Achilles tendon problems which have affected some physical activities and I find don't right themselves as they did when I was a younger man – frustrating! Also my intentions to make progress on my three proposed research activities have not been realised. Similarly a book series project with friends – loosely described as travel books – has yet to progress seriously. However although procrastination is still one of my major talents I no longer have rigid academic deadlines so I feel less pressure and shall restart the projects in my own time – rather a nice feeling!

However, I face two challenges in the near future. One is weighing up how to contribute to the local community – working with older people is one possibility on the horizon, and the other challenge is helping my partner to restructure her medical business so that she is less tied to clinical work and more able to join me on future travels. This is beginning to work, I'm delighted to report, since we are about to undertake a study tour of Mexico in the next few weeks.

Overall my message is that, so far, I have found retirement a very positive experience and as the cliché goes, 'I recommend it'!

I think we each have our own experiences and views. Another early observation is that I was late with this writing for which I apologised to the editors. Strangely enough just as when I was in full-time employment time management is still an issue. So either my procrastination, which I have carefully worked on over my academic life, is still a factor or I am busier than ever in my Third Age. Probably both are true.

# Chapter 11

# Dogs and duvets: living in rural France as a retirement project

## Alison Kirton

*'Retirement: It's nice to get out of the rat race, but you have to learn to get along with less cheese.'*

Gene Perret

> In this chapter Alison talks about how she reached the decisions to retire and to live in France. She examines her very mixed experiences of retiring in a foreign country. In order to overcome some periods of loneliness in the dark, cold winter months of her first year she describes how making her home warm and having Henri her new dog in her life turned things round. Alison discusses the importance of establishing a strong network of social groups, the difficulties of learning French and the struggle to have an authentic French experience. Despite some initial, difficult periods of adjustment Alison talks about her new adventures in a very positive way and is enjoying her new retiring life.

I am sitting in the Salle du Fete (Community Centre) of a village called Ciadoux on a cold November day with the snow-clad Pyrenees in the background. I am part of a women's sewing group, learning to make patchwork. As the group is about to finish I have to return to my little house alone. I have an existential moment, one of those sudden, deep insights into one's place in the world. I ask myself What on earth am I doing here? Do I belong? I am not sure I can live here – it is too hard.

How I came to be living in France and what my experiences tell us about retirement in a foreign country is the focus of this chapter.

I retired from working as a teacher trainer in higher education in April

2006. While I really enjoyed working with young trainees I found the higher education environment less than satisfactory. Engaged in teacher training in a university I was regarded as having escaped into an ivory tower by teachers at the chalk face in schools and viewed as, 'not a proper academic' by some of my academic colleagues. I disliked the competitive and individualistic culture as well as the pressures to write academic articles in prestigious journals without the necessary time and support.

I also felt that I was poorly managed by people who had their own pressures and priorities. This all meant that the opportunity to retire at 60 was a welcome one. I was pleased to leave what I regarded as a toxic atmosphere. I had always dreamed of buying a house in France. My mother, who was a complete Francophile, had talked a lot about buying an abandoned house and doing it up. Unfortunately my family had other pressing financial priorities so we never bought a French house. I had spent three consecutive summer holidays looking after a wonderful house in Gascony for friends. I loved the place because of the friendly local farmers and their families who were more politically active than their English counterparts. I enjoyed the wonderful local food and wine. Friends came to stay and shared with me the sun and the sunflowers and long, boozy lunches on the terrace. Such experiences made me think south-west France was the ideal place to live. Once retired I had my pension lump sum and decided to search for a little house in the sun.

## Understanding my motives?

I really do not quite understand what drove me, that summer of 2006. I knew deep down that I had to get out of London, otherwise I felt I would be tempted into accepting bits of work and would be drawn back into working again. I also wanted an adventure now that I had the time and the money to do what I wanted. I loved walking and skiing. Being near the Pyrenees would be the chance to do both these activities easily. It did seem perverse to move to a new country where I knew very few people, especially as I had a strong network of interesting friends and family in Britain. Lots of friends pointed this out to me. However, most of them were younger and working in very demanding jobs. I feared that they might not be accessible to me to do all the retirement things like walking, lunching and visiting galleries, because they were all still working.

## Feel the pain and do it anyway – buying a French house

In June 2006 I borrowed a different house in Gascony from another friend and got the names of good estate agents. I had been searching the Internet for ages so I had a good idea of what I could get for my money. I found a small house very quickly (too quickly perhaps?) which seemed such a bargain compared to the others I had seen. It had a lot of character, was the right size and had been done up tastefully by an Irish woman who has now become a friend. It was also available with all its furniture. Doing up a ruin for years was not for me! It also had central heating and an open fireplace. There were two main drawbacks: it was on a road that was busy at certain times of the day and it did not have a view of the Pyrenees. However I could imagine myself living there. It was between a small town and a village so all amenities were nearby. I was terrified and not sure it was absolutely right but I bought it anyway. After that frightening and sometimes lonely process was over I thought 'Bloody hell I now have to live in it!' I decided that my original idea of living the winter months in London and the summer ones in France would not work. I needed to be in France full-time to be part of the local community. I thought if I got good tenants for my London flat then I would not want to turf them out after six months. I then worked really hard to get my flat into a rentable state. This meant de-cluttering after years of shoving stuff into cupboards and down the cellar. The process was both cathartic and painful. It was like clearing out my old working life so that my new retired life could begin.

## A place in the sun or not!

I returned to France to take up residence in my new home. A friend came over and helped me to settle in. We washed and cleaned like Trojans and invited my neighbours, Swiss and French, for drinks. So far so good. I had decided to keep some of my teacher training work, as everyone had counselled 'don't go from working full-time to nothing'. It was when returning to my French house from one of these work trips in November 2006 that the reality of my situation suddenly hit home. The leaves had gone from the trees and the area round the house looked bare. The dark closed in at 5 p.m. and the temperature often plummeted down to minus 5. The frost reached right to the tops of the trees. Everyone seemed to hibernate, especially in the evenings; no one stirred. After living in a city like London it seemed weird that it was so dark and there were no pubs and very few restaurants that opened at night. My central heating used gas, which had to be ordered, delivered by tanker and pumped into a cistern under the ground. It was really expensive and I was anxious about using it up. I had this horrible mental image of the tank emptying. I felt I was doing battle against the cold and damp. The whole process of things like ordering gas by phone, paying utility bills, getting things repaired if they went wrong and installing broadband for my emails was a nightmare. My French was rudimentary and even if I prepared all my questions in French and wrote them down, the responses were often in very fast French, with a local accent. They were incomprehensible. I had my phone cut off because I did not understand how to fill in the payment slip. I felt it was actually dangerous in my situation to be living here but not able to speak French well. What if something went seriously wrong? I did get some help from the few friends I had made and they were wonderful. My French teacher became my 'social worker' – translating letters from the gas company, making phone calls on my behalf and trying to cheer me up. She told me later that she was very surprised that I lasted that winter. I suffered from very bad anxiety, loneliness and depression. I hated the house and did not want to get out of bed in the mornings. Christmas was coming up and I had decided to fly back to England to my family. Two friends were coming back with me for a few days for the New Year. However I then would have to spend January alone and the prospect was daunting. A friend advised me to get a dog. He advised that it would change the way I live in France and be good company. I had always wanted to own a dog but work always got in the way. I did some research about local breeds and a French acquaintance offered me a Jack Russell puppy. I was terrified to accept it as it would make me feel trapped. I would not be able to leave it to go 'home' if I needed to or to take it with me. I decided not to have it. I rang the friend who had helped me settle in and told her I was depressed and could not face the thought of January here on my own. She immediately invited me to stay with her in Shropshire for a week. That invitation made me feel better and I booked my flight. As a result I had a little energy to start to think about improving my life. I tried to build a structure to the week so that I had something for each day – sewing class on Monday, French lesson on Tuesday, market on Wednesday, walking on Thursday and then visits to friends so that the weekends were not lonely. I encouraged friends to visit and thought about starting a reading group or a walking group. These would have to be *English* groups as most of the people I made friends with were English. This was not how I imagined my life in France. Was it authentic or just being another expatriate? I needed them and it was a relief to speak English but I wanted them to be French.

### The new man in my life!

The thing that really changed my life for the better was Henri, not a romantic Frenchman (though that would have been nice!) but a terrier! When considering whether to have the Jack Russell puppy I had tried to find kennels that might take it if I wanted to go to London or skiing in the Alps. I told the woman who ran the kennels that I really wanted a Border Terrier. At the end of April I got a call from her to say that a 2-year-old terrier had been left in the kennels by a couple who said they would return for him but didn't. They had said if she could not find anyone to have him she was to have him put down. She was outraged by this and hoped I would have him. It was love at first sight! As he had spent time in the kennels it meant he could go back there if I wanted to go on holiday and it would be a holiday for him as well as he loved the owner. Getting a dog means that I now have a very clear structure in my life. It means that I get regular exercise. It means that I feel safe in the house and sleep better at night. It means that I have something else to think about and someone to talk to. People talk to you much more easily if you have a dog. It means unconditional love. Every morning I get up early and take Henri into the woods for an hour. Even if I start out in a grumpy mood I always come back feeling much better. The walk gives me time to think things through and to make decisions. The woods are a delight and so is watching Henri enjoying them. I am learning about birds and plants and mushrooms. There are some negatives of course. The fear of losing him, the vet bills and friends who do not share my enthusiasm for dogs. Being in France with a dog means you can take him into restaurants, hotels and shops – the French have always been good at subverting the rules. I do understand that not everyone sees this as an advantage.

## One year on and getting better all the time!

By the end of September 2007 I had ended my first year in France successfully. I felt much more positive after my experiences of the winter months. I had made a few really good friends, I had my lovely dog that was settling in and becoming better behaved and my French was progressing. I decided to prepare myself much better for the next winter. I bought a Hungarian goose duvet and an electric blanket. I decided to keep my fire burning 24 hours a day and only use the central heating when it was really cold. Firewood is much cheaper than gas. This meant that I had one really warm room in the house. I think it is much healthier this way and find buildings really overheated when I return to the UK. I also organised to spend three weeks in New Zealand in January and this was a great success. It was a real holiday. I spent time with really good friends. I also travelled on my own for a week very successfully. As a retired person I had thought life was one long holiday but actually I work quite hard in my house and garden as there are always things to do. It was really energising having a conventional holiday away from all responsibilities, however much they had been diminished by giving up work. I came back feeling that I could conquer the world and really positive about being in France.

## Other lessons learnt

The other thing that sustained me apart from my family and friends was the existence of the Retiring Women group. I tried to attend some meetings once I moved to France. The email system kept me in touch with both the important and mundane matters discussed by them. One of the members had said that a good mantra was to have the following three things each day: exercise, humour and achievable goals. I have found this really useful. The dog makes sure I get regular exercise but I also have kept up with my skiing and walking in the mountains. Humour, of course, but also not trying to achieve too much and being demoralised. Just one small thing a day or nothing if you want to sit in the shade and read all day. So I often set myself just one target for that day, examples would be: planting out my cosmos plants; ordering some books from Amazon; sorting out how to re-register my car here; making some plans for the weekend so that I don't spend too much time alone.

I have also learnt to be softer on myself (or I am trying). It is not possible to be able to speak French immediately or be accepted into the local French community just like that. I have to work at it and take time. I have decided to try to find some voluntary work so that I will be interacting with French people and this should make me use the language more. I think that it is very hard to learn a new language and this difficulty is often underestimated. When I do get the opportunity to speak French all evening I am completely exhausted at the end of it. My experiences here have made me understand some of the difficulties of being an 'immigrant'. These have increased my admiration for the many students I taught in London who came from other countries as small children. They learnt English quickly and succeeded in the educational system. My relationship with other English people here is tricky – on the one hand I need the useful knowledge and support they can give, but on the other I am alarmed by how easy it is to speak English and mix only with other English people most of the time. I struggle to have a more authentic experience and hope I will succeed to make friends with French people who share my left-wing and feminist values. Life in rural France is very rich. I am beginning to understand and appreciate the local democracy in the shape of the mayor and the committee that run the village affairs and organise all sorts of activities. There are fêtes when everyone meets to eat, drink and make merry. Local recitals are organised in the church. The health system in my experience is wonderful. I am now feeling much more positive and feel I will be here for at least five years! It has been a steep learning curve and an adventure.

Chapter 12

# One step forward and two back, then hopefully forward again

Diana Leonard

*'It is necessary to relax your muscles when you can. Relaxing your brain is fatal.'*

Stirling Moss

Diana's intention to step into retirement with minimum changes to her life was dashed when she was diagnosed with cancer. Her story focuses on the adjustments she needed to make. Some were very difficult, like getting through a second round of chemotherapy. Some were very positive, like acquiring a wonderful dog. In order to mark this stage of her retiring Diana planned a day with others to celebrate some of the various things she had been involved in during her working life. She also talks about other things she is looking forward to, including several holidays and considering a new phase of politically edgy writing.

My intention was to just step into 'retirement' with minimal changes to my life. I would continue doing what I enjoyed in academic life – research and writing – but give up teaching, where I felt burnt out, and almost all meetings and record-keeping. I planned to do just one project at a time, and to contribute to it fully instead of leaning on research officers. I would work in the mornings, and walk, see friends and family and do cultural things in the afternoons and evenings. I could do whatever research I wanted without having to worry about getting funding. Other professors and readers had done this before me (Tizard 2000; Tizard and Owen 2001; Reisz 2008) and it sounded ideal.

This was something of a bounce back after I was diagnosed with cancer at the end of 2002. The news came as a total shock, swiftly followed by the physical assault of six months of surgery, chemotherapy and then radiotherapy. My employers were very good about sick leave, so I did not have worries about money or job security, unlike many I encountered in waiting rooms. But the institution was much less good about discussing my workload.

Consequently, when I returned to work full-time in mid-2003, I found my job much denuded and my status diminished. It is sad to see a 'career' you have built up just melt away. But I realised reluctantly that physically I could no longer cope with a full workload. So I suggested that I take early retirement on grounds of ill-health and be brought back in for one-third time for two years, to ease myself into a new situation.

On reflection, some mentoring would have helped at this point. I was not systematic enough about actually changing my practices – nor indeed about how I thought about myself. I did not have *time* to sort things out, since a third of an academic job still seemed to involve working in the evenings and at weekends; and I did not recognise how much I cared about and was depressed by the institution's (apparently indifferent) view of me. A personal coach might have buoyed me up, made me see that things would not go on as before and kept me on a new track. The Retiring Women group was helpful, but there is an implicit limit on how much we challenge each other's choices; and I suspect my being a professor gave me a not necessarily helpful amount of licence to spout on as if I knew what I was doing. I did not set boundaries or prioritise enough. Nor did I set up a new short-term contract with a different institution (cf. several retired academics in Reisz 2008: 41) nor a position as emeritus professor in my existing university. (In fact, for some odd reason, they formally won't *let* you do this until after you have retired, ensuring you can't do any forward planning.) Nor did I get new research funding ahead of time. I see now that the future was not going to be as jolly as my first paragraph suggests unless I put some structures in place.

In the two years I was part-time, I did, however, do several spells of teaching in Pakistan and developed an interest in the country and made plans for a new (hopefully funded) research project there. I also moved my research students comfortably to a colleague who had done her own PhD with me, and continued with her as co-supervisor. I did a small research project with money from the HEFCE, and another with HEA funding. I published articles from both of these in academic journals and I reviewed more books than before. I examined several doctoral theses, did some keynote speeches at home and abroad, accepted invitations to participate in panel discussions at conferences, and was a school governor and on the advisory board of two voluntary organisations and a government advisory committee. I was also one of the editors of a textbook on changes in practical gender issues for schools. I reworked data from previous studies to fit with the topics of several specialist seminars and publications. All of which seem useful ways for a senior academic to continue to contribute her professional expertise, not only prior to but also beyond retirement.

I came to see my university more and more at a distance – through the far end of a telescope. I am still interested in its goings on and its well-being, and want to be associated with it. But it does not seem to feel the same way about its past staff and this is alienating. You have to ask for, and justify, and be granted the right to continue to be attached to a particular department.

Unlike some other contributors to this book, I thought it didn't matter if I no longer had a share of an office and access to a computer in the institution. I have always done most of my 'real work' at home and I thought I could cover my own costs just as I had previously bought the books I needed – for instance paper, printer cartridges and conference fees – though the last are now so expensive I am having second thoughts. Also I acquired a wonderful dog who does not like being left for long periods. (Actually he doesn't like being left out of anything at all.) But a sense of marginalisation, exclusion or even dismissal by the institution did not get the best from me while I was employed, nor has it helped me individually since retirement.

Although working part-time for a few years was helpful in many ways, it also kept me exposed to the drip, drip, drip of institutional indifference and the world moving onwards without me. Some in the complementary therapy field would see my having put myself back into the same stressful (for me, toxic) work situation as having contributed to my cancer re-emerging in 2006. I'm not sure – I'm more with Susan Sontag and rationalism and not blaming the victim for getting the disease. But whatever its cause(s), the disease advanced, and from late 2007, I was under pressure to have another round of chemotherapy.

Which is where I am as I write this, with a bald head, face to face with the 'elephant in the room' of retirement: whatever our best laid plans, we are getting older, and illness can upset everything at any time. Being seriously ill, and certainly getting through chemotherapy, is itself a full-time job.

However, I hope I will have some good time left. So I have been rethinking, though I am not sure I have the answers.

I do now feel the need to draw a line and then to move forward differently. I did not want a 'leaving party'. But while some of my friends have made brilliant exits – I have heard some scabrously funny and some wonderfully warm and heartfelt speeches – I would not feel comfortable as the centre of such attention. Anyway, as I said, at the time, I was not planning on 'leaving', just adjusting what I did.

Not having a public 'do' meant, however, that lots of people did not know I was 'not still there' (*sic*). And my bad prognosis – recurrent endometrial cancer may be palliated but seldom cured – suggested it would be worth taking stock. A dear friend, Miriam David, suggested she would organise a day meeting to celebrate some of the various things I had been involved with, in and around the women's movement, academia and education generally, over the last 30 or more years. And that felt just right, if ambitious.

I was touched that she cared; but one good thing about sickness is that it allows one to show emotions and to let people know they are important to you. Also, when she first mooted the idea, I had just come back from a conference where there was a general sense of anxiety in the air around retirement and her proposal seemed a way to tackle some of it and to place my biography in its context. Many of my generation were feminist activists who forged their way into higher education jobs and radically changed its curriculum, pedagogy and assessment through women's studies. We are now ceding place to younger women who, to us, may not seem to have enough of a sense of the (our!) past. But then, as Dale Spender's *There's Always Been a Women's Movement This Century* stresses, my generation didn't know what the generation before us had being doing either. But I was annoyed when people were attributed with starting things which had been going for years before they arrived on the scene. So it is important that my generation (and all others) records its history and shows there was life before Judith Butler (feminist in-joke). Also it is wonderful to have an occasion to meet up again – and maybe to stay in touch thereafter.

One of my peers, Mary Evans, commented that people keep saying to her 'You are *brave* to take early retirement.' But she knew what she was leaving in current higher education: what she didn't want to do (see her book *Killing Thinking: The death of the universities*). She now describes herself as an independent researcher, 'which is what I've been for much of my career anyway'.

This was a necessary reminder that I and many others have always looked for support mainly to those outside our own institutions – and for years in the 1970s I did not have an institution at all because my politics went ahead of me and stopped me being employed. (It was once commented in an appointment committee in a campus university that having me there 'would upset the wives' – as in make them uppity.) Feminist academics established a community outside the university for intellectual and practical support when we were very thinly spread.

To judge by the responses to the invitation to 'my day', the network is still largely there and still very supportive. Individuals just do not have as much time to devote to it. Our jobs have taken over our lives since Thatcher's reforms in the 1980s and the de- (or is it re-) professionalisation of academia. These changes destroyed some important personal and collective relationships (Maguire 2008: 51). But, heigh ho, we may become political and community-focused again when we retire – if we have the energy!

For you do not need something to substitute for the immediate status, community and companionship you have in your workplace, even if these benefits were cut across by the workaholic, competitive and repressive culture which has been built up in it over the last 20 years, as 'work becomes home and home becomes work' (Hochschild 1997).

I am therefore beginning to accept I am no longer, and will never be again, 'doing the same thing as before but without the bits I don't like'. I am somewhere different. For the moment, I plan simply to get through my current treatment, treating myself kindly and booking several holidays so as to have things to look forward to. Beyond this, I have to face up to having moved out of the university (or at least being one-third in and two-thirds out). In the future, 'if I'm spared', as my grandmother would have said, I will have to build up a happy and self-sustaining situation if I want to continue research – though with the huge advantage of no longer needing to earn a salary and not having to have external funding if I can at least cover my costs.

At the time of my retirement my university was not going to do much if anything to facilitate the continuing involvement of past faculty, despite the loss of skills and experience, especially with early retirees (MacGuire 2008). But perhaps I can gather together a group to sell this to it as a project – as did a group of academics at the Australian National University in the 1990s (ANU 2009). It is not alone in this: 'a recurring comment' in a survey of retired academic and academic-related staff 'was that universities did not recognise the actual or potential contribution of retired academics' (Tizard 2000; Tizard and Owens 2001: 268). But with imagination and organisation it could harness the potential of a wonderful, large, voluntary workforce. We could continue to bring the university prestige, support its fund-raising and develop its involvement in the local community. [But see Chapter 16 on Professional Development, which reports steps taken since Diana's retirement to exploit professors' expertise in their retirement. -Editors]

For the moment I just note how much my sense of belonging is fostered by such apparently small things as having access to an office, being kept on mailing lists and having a page on the institutional website. I am enormously encouraged when colleagues are openly pleased to see me when I attend parties, seminars and occasional meetings or use the senior common room for meals. I must build on this. (Compare a US college 'where excellent facilities and a warm welcome were available for retired researchers', which resulted in there being only a moderate decline in academic activity with age – from 58 per cent of under 75s to 41 per cent of those aged 75+. See Roman and Taietz (1967), quoted in Tizard and Owen 2001: 266.)

Failing that, I have been outside the university circle before, and know plenty who are freelance who can give me advice. Or I can buy a book or get a life coach. Who knows, it could potentially be the start of the most politically edgy and cutting-edge writing I have been allowed to do since the 1970s.

## References

Allatt, P. (2003) 'Social exclusion and the "retired" academic'. *Network: Newsletter of the British Sociological Association*, February.

ANU (2009) About the Australian National University Emeritus Faculty established in 1999, http://www.anu.edu.au/emeritus/about.html (accessed 12 March 2009).

Evans, M. (2004) *Killing Thinking: The death of the universities*. London: Continuum.

Hochschild, A. (1997) *The Time Bind: When work becomes home and home becomes work*. New York: Metropolitan Books.

Maguire, M. (2008) '"End of term": teacher identities in a post-work context'. *Pedagogy, Culture and Society*, 16(1) March, 43–55.

Newman, M. (2008) 'Retiring types in the spotlight as legacy hunters expand focus'. *Times Higher Education*, 21 August, p. 10.

Reisz, M. (2008) 'Senior service'. *Times Higher Education*, 21 February, pp. 38–41.

Roman, P. and Taietz, P. (1967) 'Organisational structure and disengagement'. *The Gerontologist*, 7, 147–60.

Spender, D. (1983) *There's Always Been a Women's Movement This Century*. London: Pandora Press.

Tizard, B. (2000) 'When are retired academics not…?' *Times Higher Education Supplement*, 24 March, pp. 34–5.

Tizard, B. and Owen, C. (2001) 'Activities and attitudes of retired university staff'. *Oxford Review of Education*, 27(2), 253–70.

Chapter 13

# Retiring backwards

## Caroline Lodge

'Half our life is spent trying to find something to do with the time we have rushed through life trying to save.'

Will Rogers

Caroline's story of retiring tells of her awareness that preparation was a good thing, and tells also of her difficulties in knowing what or how to prepare. Not yet quite retired, Caroline found a way to think about the transitions from working life by visualising her preferred future life, planning backwards from this and by learning from the Retiring Women group's activities and deliberations about retiring.

My story of retiring is about indecision and about finding some ways of making necessary decisions and the grounds on which to make those decisions. I have been accused of procrastination. It has felt more like a combination of ambivalence and inability to make decisions. The solution I found was to work backwards, as my story reveals.

In my early fifties I woke up one morning with the realisation that my job as a lecturer in education at the Institute of Education would probably be my last. When I began work it stretched on into a seemingly endless future. But with the passing of years I have come to see that at some point my working life will not continue as the main or only organising feature of my life. With this insight came another. I had a degree of flexibility and choices about the transition and time to plan a good transition from my working life. The choices I needed to make included these:

- When should I go?
- Should I go all at once or, like other colleagues, phase out my working life?

- Where should I live?
- What might I do with my time?
- Would I have enough money for whatever I chose to do?

I am truly glad for all the choices I have about retiring, even if I find the decisions hard to make. I am not going to be a worker summarily tipped out with a new watch or pen, on the day of my sixtieth or sixty-fifth birthday – going 'over a cliff' as someone recently described his experience of retiring. I have earned enough in my life to have some choices about where I live, and my health is sound, which allows me to consider a range of activities. Nor am I a stranger to making decisions and changes. About 12 years before I had decided that I did not want to be a secondary headteacher for the remainder of my working life.

But the choices about retiring presented me with a very big problem: I had no criteria upon which to base my decisions. Like many women, many of the decisions in my life, including my working life, have been made with pressing imperatives implicated in my relationships with others, children, ageing parents and partners. But at the time when I was waking up to approaching retirement I only had loose ties – healthy or deceased parents, an adult daughter, a loosely coupled relationship with a man.

The book I would have liked to help me think about these issues did not exist then (I hope this is it). But the one thing I did get from reading about retiring was, PLAN AHEAD. Planning implies a clear idea of the steps you want to take. I was going round in circles.

After floundering for a while I did take several sensible steps. I began to talk to friends, I asked for some professional guidance, I joined the Retiring Women group and I spent a good deal of time thinking about the meaning of retirement for me, and what I could best do with the wealth of choices and experiences opening up to me. Some of these strategies have been more helpful than others. Those processes that have involved other people have been more productive.

## Strategy 1: Learning from the experiences of friends

It does not seem to me that there are many very good role models for retiring, and especially for women. I have some friends who have retired. Three close women friends had the time and pace of retiring set by their health problems, all earlier than they might have chosen. A close male friend (just a year younger than me) decided to retire from headship, in order to pay more attention to his ageing mother as well as to look after his own health problems. He had a great plan, to see all the people on his Christmas card list in the first year of his retirement. He loved walking and died of a heart attack in Italy, on a walking holiday with a friend. He died within a year of his retirement. I still miss him.

My learning from the experiences of others included useful information about claiming pensions, about the pleasures of flexible time, about the opportunities of the next phase of life. It also confirmed my view that I needed to continue preparing by thinking about what retiring might mean to me. These are helpful learnings (much as the stories in this book are intended to be), but this strategy did not make a significant contribution to help me to make those important decisions.

## Strategy 2: Professional guidance

There were two strands to this strategy. First I attended a pre-retirement course (two days) with the Life Academy. I found it hard to fit in with the other participants. In the first place, I was not yet 55 but most of the participants were very recently retired or about to retire within a month or so. They did not seem to me to be taking the course in advance of retiring, and so I stood out. Second, I am a woman, independent, confident, with a long career in education. There was only one other independent woman on the course. The other women were wives of retirees. And third, all the other participants worked outside London, had grandchildren, belonged to golf clubs. My life was not in their pattern. The course was helpful in some ways. It helped me see that planning was a good thing and that I was thinking about the right kinds of things. But it did not help me with my choices.

The second professional guidance strategy was to have a couple of sessions with a work coach. I approached my colleague responsible for professional development, who provided and funded the coaching (see Chapter 16). I called him my retirement coach and eventually retired him after two sessions. Both sessions were helpful, and they resulted in reducing the number of days I worked. To some extent this was in order to prepare for a life less dominated by work, but it also allowed me to gain more control over my working life, to do some consultancy work so my salary was not drastically reduced, and to make it possible to have time for walking, reading and writing and spending time with friends during the 'working week'. This was a significant move, but the final when and why and how of retiring were still not yet touched.

## Strategy 3: The Retiring Women group

The Retiring Women group has been very helpful. In the first place, the members were all women with whom I had something in common: a career in education, working at the Institute for the final phase of their working life, many did not have orthodox patterns to their lives and all were thinking about retiring. The women had a variety of experiences of approaching retiring, and all of us were concerned to learn together about what it would mean to each of us and how we could support each other.

Within the group we find support, for action, for deliberation, for creativity and for activities not associated directly with retiring but that enhance the quality of our lives. Monthly meetings have meant that you never loose touch with the potential for a check on your well-being and deliberations and plans. The residential sessions have helped move us forward as a group and individually, through focused and deep explorations. (See Chapters 2 and 3 for an account of the group and what we learned about running the group.)

Through the work of the group the choices for retiring, about when, how, where and so forth, have been linked to other aspects of my life, and I have a warm and secure forum to consider implications, alternatives and to move towards some tentative decisions. Now that I can see that these choices are interrelated I have found it helpful to think about how I want to live my life in five or even ten years.

In our first residential session I learned three important things that have stayed with me and been an important part of my thinking. I came to realise that I could start my thinking about the best of what I wanted it to be, and then plan for that, rather than starting where I am now and plan my immediate next steps. I call this retiring backwards. I came to this understanding as a result of a visualisation activity at that weekend (and this was reaffirmed two years later after a second visualisation activity in a different context). We were asked to think about being retired and that it was a good experience, and to visualise how it felt, how it looked, who we were with, and so on.

I could see myself in a life that was productive, appreciated and very involved with other people – people I cared about and liked. In this future I was physically and intellectually active, healthy, supported by a number of warm friends and family members and in turn adding something to their lives and those of others beyond my intimate circle. This was a future worth preparing for. And I could plan and realise significant steps towards ensuring that I moved steadily towards the life I envisaged.

I re-engaged with backward planning recently in a different context. I was practising skills with some fellow work coaches and we were again invited to consider how we wanted our life to be five years ahead. Then we visualised three years ahead, then one, then six months. The final step was to plan what needed to be done between each stage. I have just come through my first six months, which has done two important things. First it has confirmed my general vision for my future in five years' time, and also given me a sense of achievement as I have made considerable progress with the practical things I need to do to achieve the life I want. Now as I move into my second six-month period, I review the overall direction, and then the interim plans. The major shift is that I intend to finish paid work at my institution sooner than in the first plan.

My second learning was that retiring is only the next stage in my life, not the final stage. There will be more stages in future. This is an important learning, that life has meaning in one's sixties and that that meaning will probably change through the subsequent stages and I will develop different meanings as I go along. I think that I had believed that death is the stage after work, after a short interval called retirement. I came to see that so long as I am blessed with good health this is unlikely to be the case.

My third learning was the understanding that I need different communities. In part this helps me understand my reluctance to take any final steps. My work community is important to me: socially, productively and in terms of the respect I receive. Like many others facing retiring, I have had to consider how to replace the community of work. I have other communities, of course, including family and friends. I now have a grandson and my future vision includes him. Oliver represents an extension of my most precious community, my immediate family. And since our first Retiring Women residential weekend I have pursued a deliberate strategy of building up and refreshing my other communities. This has involved sharing activities with friends, embracing new friends, creating new social opportunities.

The group has helped in a number of other ways too. Over the years the group has discussed alternative forms of occupation: volunteering and part-time work as well as family responsibilities. My emerging plans for occupying my time have been informed by these discussions. I am also clearer about some of the things that I do and do not want to do. I admire the members of the group who have embraced moving abroad and taking on new responsibilities in dogs. I have much to learn about being a grandmother, new skills, undertaking volunteer work, taking holidays in retirement and so on.

Since I began to think about retiring I have been getting more and more tired. Like many of my friends of a similar age, I am wondering why work has not become easier with greater experience and wisdom. Rather the struggles seem depressingly familiar, the burdens repetitive and the pleasures compensate less well. More and more I like days when I am not at work, when I can walk, meet friends, read, go to cultural events, learn to sail, look for new houses. And the occasions when I feel valued by the institution in which I work remain as few as ever. So why not leave?

I am now making my decisions, I have an evolutionary plan. It starts backwards. In five years' time I will be volunteering, living in two places, grandparenting and happy with this new stage of life. At this point in my progress I have come to see that to take time, to do it backwards, has been good. This has enabled me to feel calmer, more agency about my future, more purpose in making decisions and to face up to the losses of retiring with more equanimity. This means that I can now see the road there as full of adventures that I anticipate with lots of enthusiasm.

# Chapter 14

# A conversation with Ted Mercer, looking back twenty years

*'Retirement is wonderful. It's doing nothing without worrying about getting caught at it.'*

Gene Perret

> We asked Ted Mercer to look back at the experience of retiring, after 20 years. Ted is a former primary headteacher and inspector in the education service. He reflects on the physical changes that he experienced at retiring, and the need to think about occupying the time that is free. He had no choice 20 years ago about when he retired, but found that he was pleased to leave the pressures of his work at that time, and to return for a while in a part-time consultant role.

I had forgotten a lot of this, and it caused a bit of upheaval to remember it. It is 20 years since I retired and much of what you asked me about had gone to sleep, was difficult to recapture after all this time...

*When did you retire? At what age? Did you choose to go at that time or did you have no choice?*

I had no choice about when to retire. You went on your sixty-fifth birthday. There was no preparation to speak of. The accounts office asked you to come and see them and sort out your pension. On the day, I had a meeting with some colleagues in the afternoon and then I left.

*What was your career before retiring?*

I had had 17 years in primary schools, the last five as a headteacher. Then I worked for 12 years in a college of education, and was head of department for the last three years. Then I had 11 years as an inspector with the ILEA [Inner London Education Authority], finishing as a district inspector. I could have taken early retirement when Sidney Webb College closed, when I was in my late fifties, but I took a significant cut in salary to become an inspector with the ILEA, anticipating that I would get back to my previous salary level by the time I got to retirement age – which I did.

*How did you feel about retiring at that time?*

I don't recall a dominant feeling, such as 'I can't wait', which other people seemed to feel. It was pleasant to think that other people would take up the pressures and confrontation that I was working with. This was 1988, and they were difficult times for people working in the ILEA in County Hall. It was a time of hard graft, with conflict as a way of life. There were always difficulties. I had set up three teams of more experienced teachers to work in schools, at the headteachers' invitations. They got called Mercer's Hit Squad, and some heads did not want them.

The more experienced members of staff, such as myself, were frequently called upon to deal with problems. I remember three: *The Sun* had picked up a story about a school where the teachers wanted to have an assembly about Nelson Mandela, who was being freed from Robben Island at the time. This was one story in a series of stories about the loony left.

Then there was a problem with a school in Islington, where I had to intervene because of problems between the headteacher and chair of governors. My report was leaked and was reported on the front page of *The Independent*.

And then there was the infant school headteacher, who was having a sit-in with parents over something that the ILEA was doing, of which he didn't approve. I remember I was at the Geffrye Museum in Hackney when a call came from Peter Newsom [Chief Education Officer of the ILEA] who told me to go and sort it out.

When you look back you often remember the mistakes or the things that you wish you had done differently. But it is good when you meet people who thought well of your work.

It was a difficult time, the ILEA officers found themselves in the middle of lots of politics and it was nice to be relieved of this.

*Any thoughts about the changes retiring brought to your life as you look back now?*

For one month I did nothing, and it felt like a long holiday. Then I began to feel, 'what do I do now?' I was asked to go back to complete follow-up work to the authority's inspection reports. This meant working three days a week as a consultant, meeting with headteachers and governors to review their progress. I had no other demands. I really enjoyed this because there was no pressure. I did this right up until the ILEA came to an end in March 1990. It was good to keep in touch, and to do something useful and meaningful.

After that I took up French classes, and then cookery, which I only gave up in 1997. Another thing I did was visiting for the London Pension Fund to support pensioners in my home area. I met engineers, draughtsmen, all the range of people who are employed by a large authority. Not many of them needed assistance, the only person who really needed my help was the widow of a lighterman.

*Any advice for people considering retiring?*

I think it is important to find meaningful employment or occupation for what can become a lot of free time. This can ease you gradually into another way of life, for when your body's metabolism changes. I do believe that this happens when you retire, and you also need to work at your clarity of mind and your linguistic ability.

Chapter 15

# Into the airlock

## Alex Moore

*'I am a free man. I feel as light as a feather.'*

Javier Cuellar

Alex is in the process of assessing and reassessing his life up to retirement, to where he stands now. In describing the retiring process he finds the metaphor of the airlock helpful – a gradual adjustment from one environment to another very different one. The airlock constitutes a rather scary, solitary kind of place but one that offers security and safety.

### 1

After a career mostly devoted to 18 years as a schoolteacher followed by a further 18 in higher education, I decided to take early retirement in April 2008. I was 61 at the time, and had intended to go a year earlier, but the university at which I was a head of department was going through a complex restructuring process, an important period was coming up in which the research activities were to be judged (the Research Assessment Exercise) and it seemed appropriate to stay on for the extra year.

For many years – most of my working life, in fact – retirement had represented (as it must do to many people) something of an ambivalent prospect. When times were bad, it would take on the aspect of a happy haven at the end of a particularly arduous journey: a celebratory moment followed by a life free to do the things I had always wanted to do rather than being constantly deflected and preoccupied (as it had always felt) by the demands of others. When things were going well, on the other hand, it adopted (when it showed itself at all) a very different aspect: an indication that old age had arrived, that the best of life was past, that the days were depressingly and uncontrovertibly numbered, that the chance and time to achieve were gone.

In the event, neither aspect has come to the fore. Not yet, anyway. I haven't dwelt very much, if at all, on the 'time and tide' stuff; nor have I popped the champagne corks or immersed myself in a flurry of social and creative activity. Retirement may, still, be many if not all of the things I might have hoped it would be: it may give me the time I have often craved to spend more time with my family, including my two recently arrived granddaughters, to write novels and poetry, to travel the world, to find out more about the wondrous workings of the universe, to learn Spanish and Chinese, to get fit, to hone my photographic skills, to rediscover the healthy art of relaxation, and – yes – to continue to research and write about my specialist academic area (education) free of the ever-heavier burdens of bureaucracy. But at the moment, admittedly just a few short weeks in, it is more a time of coming to grips, of filling my days with self-imposed, tuggy-blanket chores, of learning to cope without the given structures and routines, and, in particular, of reluctantly coming to terms with the awful possibility (more of this later) that 'going to work', rather than being the distraction I had always taken it for, might actually have served a more hidden purpose of keeping more adventurous, perhaps more 'meaningful' activities on the back burner.

What I'm saying, I suppose, is that before I can feel the promised liberation (please let it be that, rather than the feared demoralisation!), I am experiencing the need – the inevitability, perhaps – to go through a rather uncomfortable process of assessing and reassessing the life that has led up to retirement, to where I stand now. In particular, I need to learn to put failure, and a sense of failure, into a perspective that renders it tolerable, to be more positive about what I have achieved as identified by other people, and to avoid filling the remainder of my days with yet more half-hearted projects whose only purpose is one of endless procrastination. I'm aware, even as I write, that this bit is probably 'just me' (the 'me' that retirement, as an important aside, is providing the space and time to discover), and not to be taken too seriously; but it may help to clarify the curiously muddled, confused response to retirement that immediately beset me once the magical moment had arrived.

This is something of a summary that needs filling out. What follows is the 'story so far': an attempt, rather sketchy (for which I apologise), to articulate the awkward questions that retirement has laid bare for me, and my first uneasy steps towards a promised land that I still hope will not disappoint. This may not, immediately, be very uplifting for the reader: not the celebratory piece I had initially imagined it would be. But, though racked with self-exploration, I cannot say that I am any less happy than when I was in full-time paid employment, and it's very reassuring to hear people tell me how well and how relaxed I now seem. Already, the tyrannical, persistent pressure of deadlines has weakened significantly enough for me to contemplate chucking it out altogether. And already that long, shadowy list of 'non-work' jobs, to do with parenting and home ownership, that had rubbed away at the edges of my consciousness adding to the anxiety and panic of too much to do in too little time, has reduced down to the extent that I can feel reasonably reassured at completing or part-completing one such activity per day. Time is still an issue, of course: inevitably so, when one reaches a certain age. But at least, now, its too rapid passing is sweetened and leavened by the rediscovery of (a not wholly illusory sense of) choice.

## 2

To be honest about it, I never really wanted to go to work in the first place, in the sense of having 'a job', so that retirement – what happens at the end of 'the job' – had never really been an issue until well after the non-job fantasy had evaporated. As a sixth-form student at a local grammar school, the only careers to which I'd given serious consideration all involved fame, fortune, plenty of free time and total job satisfaction, followed by a void, of unspecified duration, to be filled by all manner of leisure activities, stretching ahead of me from some point in my mid-thirties until I kicked the bucket (probably at some point in my seventies). Footballer, novelist, poet, rock star: all these careers (and it was always 'careers', never 'professions') had been entertained and even trained for during my teenage years (Sunday League football team, rhythm guitarist in pub band, endless penning of poems, pseudo-autobiographical clips of teenage angst), and they continued to be so when, at the height of flower power, I read and lounged and drank my way through three years at laid-back, bucolic Exeter University. I received no careers advice before leaving university with my 2:1 (Hons) English degree, and so still had no grand plan regarding work/end of work when I was forced, through penury rather than conscience, into the job market in the summer of 1968. The only plan I did have – if plan is not too grandiose a concept – was to return to my parents' home and find temporary work that would keep me solvent until such time as my chosen career could get underway. By now, three years of alcohol and nicotine abuse had effectively removed from my shortlist of possible careers the footballer option, and my youthful confidence at becoming a rock star had been seriously dented by a growing recognition of my lack of musical talent (How had I not picked up on this earlier?). However, fuelled by my relative success as an English student and a perhaps arrogant view that not all the literature I had been asked to study had been as great as it had been cracked up to be, I had not given up on the literary option, and the idea of becoming a successful novelist was to become an abiding – one might say, a consuming – ambition for much of the rest of my working (non-novel-writing) life.

In a sense, this was all, in itself, a little strange, in that I had been brought up in an environment (a working-class council estate in South East London) in which 'careers' and 'jobs' (albeit as dire necessities), in all their aspects had tended to enter into the minds of young people and their families from a very early age. That I had somehow escaped this preoccupation was in part due to my own parents' grand and unlikely aspirations for me, which themselves did not look beyond attending three successful years at university and thus becoming only the second person on the entire estate to hold a university degree – the other being my older sister, herself an earlier beneficiary of that same astonishing faith. After the achievement of this goal, it was assumed (I imagine) that the rest of my life would simply take care of itself. With a university degree, the world was bound to be my oyster; it was not a question of whether I would get a 'good' job (i.e. one that combined good pay with a high degree of 'respectability') but which, from an array of possible good jobs, I would eventually opt for.

All this is by way of explaining that (and how) I came to embark on a working life which, in retrospect and probably at the time, seems totally without plan or shape and from which thoughts of retirement remained missing until a point was reached – not very long before the event itself – at which I realised that none of my preferred careers (over the years, these had expanded, in a come-and-go sort of way, to include photographer, politician, journalist and TV presenter – 'professions', I suppose – though the list was always headed by novelist) was ever going to materialise. Gradually it dawned on me that the work I had been undertaking to keep the wolf from the door (an ever larger and hungrier wolf, as children and mortgages arrived on the scene) had actually become, by some act of stealth and deception, my career, and that the end would not be a break from the provisional but a much larger and much harder-to-get-to-grips-with change of life. That career was in education – the very thing I had probably most sought to escape from once I had left university. Like many other jobs I had undertaken in my early twenties (shelf-filler, warehouseman, trainee manager for a major insurance company), teaching had also started as a temporary fix while I waited for the real work to kick in. I had not been trained as a teacher, had never seriously thought of teaching as a possible long-term job for myself, and had only started as a supply teacher to cover for someone else's summer-term sick leave. This in itself had constituted little more than an escape from the insurance work, which I had hated, and had I not been offered a permanent post at the end of my term's supply work no doubt I would simply have moved on and away into some other temporary work.

Eighteen years and three schools later, I was still in school-teaching, despite having had two one-year breaks in futile pursuit of the prize-winning novel, and perhaps it was at the end of this period that the truth(s) of the matter finally began to sink in: first, a grudging acknowledgement that, despite what may have appeared to be a life of professional achievement in the eyes of others (I had progressed during the 18 years from English teacher to head of year to head of faculty to senior teacher), I was probably never going to pursue the career I had always wanted and (fancifully?) assumed would bring the fulfilment and justification I craved; second, I had, in any event, almost unbeknownst to myself, come to love teaching and to develop a serious interest in education. At the time, this awareness seemed to have taken me to a crossroads, the choice of direction depending partly on circumstances, partly on the ever fluctuating readings of my situation. These latter varied from (a) I had frittered away the best part of my life through endless post-ponements and digressions, to (b) I had been deluding myself that I could ever be the novelist I thought I wanted to be, that such a career would not have brought the craved satisfaction and justification, that my enduring *dis*-satisfaction with life was not work-dependent but part of who I was (and perhaps always would be), and that I should stick with something that I knew, deep down, I was not only pretty good at but could actually do something positive for other people.

It was at this point, almost accidentally (again…), via an MA course at the Institute of Education that had led me into a PhD, that I had entered higher education – a place I was to remain in for the next 18 years. It was a compro-mise of sorts – carrying on teaching and being involved in education while hav-ing the time and the opportunity to write (not novels, but they could wait now, fame having long since receded as a requirement of my chosen work); however, it proved to be a very happy one that did not quite remove the dissatisfaction but did provide abundant compensations. The desire to write creatively did not leave me, but the need was met well enough, and my research and teaching filled me with such stories and ideas that I found myself writing more – and probably more usefully – than I had ever done before.

My attitude to retirement also underwent a considerable change during this period – and not simply, I think, because of its ever-quickening approach. I began to think about it quite *seriously* for the first time – even to plan for it – and, now, not so much in terms of one final opportunity to achieve immortal-ity (for such, I now realised, was the real motivation behind the dream) as to enjoy that life of freedom and choice – that happy haven – that I referred to at the start of these musings – recognising, I think, that only through such enjoy-ment could the negative aspects of retirement be overridden. (I no longer craved immortality, but that didn't mean I was happy about growing old and dying.) This change of perspective was probably fuelled by the fact that, as I grew older, I came into increasing contact with already-retired people, most of them full of the joys of a second Spring. Ironically perhaps, given my history, I was among the last of my group of old school friends to take retirement. Most of them, and mostly voluntarily, had quit full-time employment (in several cases, employment altogether) in their early fifties, and had already been ladies and gentlemen of leisure for the best part of a decade before, for me, it had even re-emerged as a serious possibility. Almost to a person they spoke positively of the change: of a sense of liberation, of recovering a life, of 'wondering how they had ever found the time to go to work'. Some – mostly those for whom the decision had been less than wholly voluntary, who had spent the majority of their working lives as the principal breadwinner, who still had children at home or going through university – talked of feelings of 'emasculation'; but these constituted a very small minority, and though in one key regard (I still had two children at home, both with aspirations to attend university) my circumstances were not dissimilar, I had quickly assumed that I was likely to identify much more strongly with the former group. Having taken out a subscription to 'Friends reunited', I even discovered, though why I should have found this surprising I don't really know, that the friends I had hung out with as a child on the council estate had all retired and seemed to be enjoying a lifestyle that I could only look upon with envy. These were not people who had been to university, or who had ever planned for early retirement, or who had 'money in the family', and they had been brought up surrounded by the same attitudes to work as I had; and yet somehow they, too, had managed happily to unburden themselves of the toady work with absolutely no sense of regret or failure. On the contrary, they spoke with some pride of the lifestyles they now enjoyed after – in most cases – 35 years of hard graft, regaling me tantalisingly with stories of their latest winter holidays, their overseas properties and their golf handicaps. Why, I wondered, was I still in work when I had never wanted to be in the first place? As soon as I could afford it, I wanted some of this action: I deserved it; I wanted to enjoy the world before it was too late!

## 3

As other new 'retirees' will know, it is not, of course, always that easy. Freedom (from work, as from anything) can be a two-edged sword. On the one hand, it is, without doubt, a great privilege to wake up in the morning with a rare and real sense of choice over what to do with the day, with the week and beyond (not complete choice, of course, with a house to maintain and bills to be paid and shopping to be done; and not quite the same, either, for those many, many people for whom retirement brings more difficulties, financial and otherwise, than it solves: and yes – we are the lucky ones!). On the other hand, you do, inevitably, over the years become 'institutionalised'. By that, I don't mean you become inseparably attached to a specific institution (though I have seen this happen); rather, that you can become overly attached and used to the institution of paid employment, of labouring together with other people, of getting up and going to a place of work in the morning and coming home at night, of completing tasks mostly set by somebody else. Like the rescued animal released again into the wild, it is always going to be a tad scary living without all that – in a world without that amount of 'structure', of security, of predictability – and it does take some getting used to.

It's a change that also gives pause for thought. In my case – perhaps typically, perhaps not – it has led to a particularly disturbing and somewhat depressing set of thoughts revolving in ever decreasing circles around one central question: What if paid employment was not what I have always taken it for? What (say) if it was not a prison to which I had been condemned and from which I could not, despite several attempts, escape, but a safe haven (the safe haven that retirement was supposed to be), in which I could blame my lack of success (as a writer, footballer, rock star, etc.) on circumstances rather than on an inherent lack of talent or determination? What if, hard though I had thought I was working, it had (for me) been the lazy option?

This may sound daft, but for me it has been a deep and genuine problem. In the weeks and months leading up to retirement, I had wondered if I would experience a certain loss of identity on quitting full-time employment – a feeling of no longer contributing to society, of uselessness if you like. That may happen, though it hasn't yet – partly, perhaps, because in addition to doing 'things for myself' I have chosen to return to paid employment on a part-time basis as well as 'contributing' in a number of ways outside work, both in giving more time to my own family and in carrying on with writing and research projects in my own time. What I have felt, though – oddly, perhaps? – is a sense of loss of a different kind, that I can only describe as a loss of fantasy. (I was going to say, a loss of hope or the loss of a dream – but that sounds a lot worse, a lot more despairing than it actually is.) What I mean by this is that all the while I had been working, even after my attitude to retirement had changed, I could tell myself that the job was temporary, that one day I would have the time to do some of the other stuff that had meant so much to me. All that did come, immediately, was a recognition (perhaps a mis-recognition) of everything I had *failed* to achieve, only heightened by that sense of 'too lateness', of time running out (that continues to play around the edges of experience even though it declines to take centre stage). Perhaps work had, after all, been a friend rather than a foe – had kindly masked from me that which had made me unhappy since I had undertaken paid employment in the first place. It had not been the dire necessity of work that had depressed at all – though I had allowed it to seem that way; it had been the fact that I had never been good enough to achieve those things that I had set out to achieve. And now, with work gone, there was no longer any getting away from it.

**4**

The good news is that all this appears now, in the words of the song, to have been a (silly) phase I was going through.

Some weeks ago, I was approached by two female colleagues, one recently retired, one working towards it, and asked if I would be interested in contributing a chapter to a book they were planning to edit on the subject of retiring. This felt like quite a strange request at the time: not because it was in any way odd to make such an invitation, but because it was so long since I had been asked to undertake any writing activity of this kind. I must confess that my speedy agreement had far more to do with my respect for these colleagues – including a conviction that anything they thought was a good idea almost certainly would be – than with any immediate sense of what it might offer to myself or to anybody else.

In the event, it has proved a curiously therapeutic exercise – like all good therapy helping me through and beyond a difficult transition in much quicker time than I could reasonably have hoped had I been left to my own devices. The pressure I was putting on myself (the pressure to 'achieve', or perhaps the pressure of self-accusation at *not having achieved*) has gone: it has ebbed away as I have thought about it and written about it, until now it appears as a vestige, an echo of that institutionalisation I remarked on earlier: the insertion of one production-related stress into the void left by the sudden removal of others. I'm more relaxed now, and I have moved away from the knee-jerk need to be doing something for the approval of others. I have started writing again – both academically and fictionally – for the pleasure it gives me and because I hope (rather than desire) that it will be of interest and perhaps help to others. In fact, now that the pressure to produce has been lifted, I have become more productive than I ever was (a phenomenon that may well be linked to another, Robert Browningesque paradox, that as death approaches so the desire for immortality recedes). Perhaps much of my working life *was* a digression, an endless sequence of displacement activities. Perhaps I was right about that. But isn't that what life is anyway? And why should it be a concern? A big difference now is that, instead of living with one eye constantly squinting at a future whose image is never better than fuzzy, I can enjoy what each day brings (and, let's be honest, fellow pensioners, as time slips away that's probably the only way *to* live!).

In making sense of all this, and this remains, as will have become very evident, a work in progress, and in my efforts to foreground and so to soften the impact of my struggles on my friends and immediate family, I have found the metaphor of the airlock helpful. The airlock – in some ways, similar to the canal lock – is the space entered by the astronaut before stepping out into space or back into the ship. Stepping out, the space, initially full of breathable air, is sealed off from the ship and from the space outside and gradually emptied until it provides a 'match' with the lack of atmosphere of space. The outer door is then opened for the astronaut to complete the journey out of the ship. Returning, the opposite process occurs, the airlock being sealed following the astronaut's return into it before being filled with breathable air that matches the air inside the ship. The thing about the airlock is that it does not exist solely to protect the astronaut – to provide a gradual adjustment from one environment, one atmospheric pressure to another, very different one; it has an even more important function of protecting the ship itself and its other occupants – for to open the ship's hatch without the airlock would be to release all the breathable air into the void of space.

In relation to retirement – my retirement I suppose I should say – the metaphor works in two ways, depending on whether I view myself as the astronaut (in which case, the ship and its occupants represent family, close friends, a lifestyle that is partly shared with others) or as the ship (in which case, the astronaut is a part of me, an experience, perhaps, or a set of feelings). Either way, the airlock constitutes a rather scary, nervy, solitary kind of place in which, despite the availability of electronic communication, one is always alone, cocooned, slightly detached – but it's a place that also offers security and safety. Its occupancy is temporary: there is nothing in here to sustain life for very long, and it always has the character of a halfway house, an interim, provisional space, in which one is always on the way from one place to another.

Stepping into the airlock (rather than leaping straight out into space, for example), also offers the opportunity – the possibility – of return. And perhaps, in the end, that is why the metaphor – and the approach it suggests – is so appealing. When I think about it, its provisionality, its air of temporariness and deferral, sits remarkably well as an approach to retirement with the defining characteristics of the working life that has preceded it. At the moment, retirement itself still seems like a bit of a void – welcoming in its endless possibilities, but simultaneously frightening in its emptiness and lack of recognisable reference points. That perspective will no doubt change, and with it the metaphors and the ways of seeing and feeling it. Then, the airlock won't be necessary any more. I will have completed the transition, will have made my choices and settled into the life for which I have opted.

The alternatives aren't such appealing ones, and not too seriously to be entertained. They are to remain inside the airlock indefinitely (a short-term response, that can only lead to some form of death), or to turn around and re-enter the ship. But all this is up for grabs. And I'm beginning to like it that way. The champagne is on ice, anyway, which can't be bad.

# Section 3

# Supporting and celebrating retiring

This section focuses on very practical issues. The three chapters consider retiring as an aspect of professional development (including a set of reflective activities); recurring financial themes; and reasons to be cheerful (a list of many of the benefits, allowances and privileges of becoming older). An Appendix lists a fairly random, annotated bibliography identifying novels, poetry, books on transitions and health, and other sources of information.

**One Art**
by Elizabeth Bishop

*The art of losing isn't hard to master;*
*so many things seem filled with the intent*
*to be lost that their loss is no disaster.*

*Lose something every day. Accept the fluster*
*of lost door keys, the hour badly spent.*
*The art of losing isn't hard to master.*

*Then practice losing farther, losing faster:*
*places, and names, and where it was you meant*
*to travel. None of these will bring disaster.*

*I lost my mother's watch. And look! my last, or*
*next-to-last, of three loved houses went.*
*The art of losing isn't hard to master.*

*I lost two cities, lovely ones. And, vaster,*
*some realms I owned, two rivers, a continent.*
*I miss them, but it wasn't a disaster.*

*—Even losing you (the joking voice, a gesture*
*I love) I shan't have lied. It's evident*
*the art of losing's not too hard to master*
*though it may look like*
*(*Write *it!) like disaster.*

Reprinted from *The Complete Poems 1927–1979*,
published by Farrar, Straus and Giroux, LLC.

Chapter 16

# Professional development for retiring

## Jacqui MacDonald

*'If you rest, you rust.'*

Helen Hayes

This chapter is written from a professional development perspective, not by someone who is retiring. It takes the view that best practices in planning for retiring are precisely those that are important in planning any stage in professional or career development. Jacqui sees the process of retiring as just as important as any other aspect of professional learning and suggests that any organisation has a responsibility to provide support for individuals who are contemplating changes to their working lives.

The chapter addresses several themes and related activities, continuities and changes in retiring, the value of imagining a perfect retirement, the importance of planning, steps to consider along the way, getting support, networking, and considering paid and non-paid work.

The activities can be carried out by individuals thinking about retiring or for groups of people meeting together to get support in making decisions about their futures.

### Introduction

For the last ten years I have been the head of staff development in the organisation in which a number of this book's contributors have been employed. Over the last three years it has been rewarding to observe members of the Retiring Women group (see Chapters 2 and 3) develop and take on the challenges of this particular stage of their lives. This has been an exciting example of collective professional development – an enriching and transforming context for learning. Through the Retiring Women group's activities we have learned so much about the process of retiring and in this chapter I want to capture some important themes for professional development in retiring.

## Recurring themes in retiring

In reading through the chapters of this book a number of issues emerge in relation to professional learning. I now consider these and then present a number of related activities.

The first of these issues is to do with continuities and changes in retiring. The prospect of retiring may be scary for some as they feel that everything they do will change or what provides support and structure in their life will disappear. But this is not necessarily so. Thinking about what is important in work life can provide a way of seeing what people need to retain in some way. What individuals value in their work life needs to be made explicit to ensure that when they stop working these aspects are still part of their lives. For example, writers in this book value being challenged intellectually, value structure in their day and value the social life that comes through work. As the working environment can often provide rich experiences for people a consideration of how to continue these activities after people have retired is really important.

The second theme is to do with imagination. My advice to anyone thinking about retiring would be 'Dare to dream'. By this I mean explore the life you want to live and live it. We read in Caroline's chapter (13) how imagining her perfect retirement provided a trigger for a structured decision-making process. We read that Alison dreamed about living in France and her dream came true. In reading others' stories we know that retirement can be rather daunting as it may be a shift from someone's usual comfort zone, but change in retirement doesn't have to be that different from the present. It might only mean just a few tweaks as some of the writers in this book describe.

However, planning is crucial in all cases. My mantra is: if you fail to plan you plan to fail – while recognising an element of serendipity in all that we do and experience. In Eileen's chapter (6) we even read how she plans for spontaneity! I believe that you need to treat your approach to retirement like any professional opportunity and this needs a plan. This is a time for strategic thinking; you need to work out a timescale and start taking action now. Retiring as an aspect of professional development requires the individual to start planning early, develop strategies, revise the plan, and consult with others, perhaps a coach or a critical friend.

The fourth theme is about the steps needing to be taken along the way, in other words breaking down the plan in order to achieve it. One step may be to do with carrying out research or enquiring about something (such as volunteering) or to check out one's finances with an adviser. A number of contributors talked about the importance of this. The development of new interests may require finding out about classes, or where to learn a language before travelling abroad, as in Alex's and Jennifer's cases.

Across the book we read about the importance of getting support. The Retiring Women set up their group in order to build a community of people who share the same focus and the same values. In other chapters we read about other communities being started or developed. One of the biggest fears in retiring and getting older is about losing human contact so it is crucial to do some work on maintaining and building communities.

A linked theme to the one above is networking. Networking is about how to use formal and informal networks and organisations. This is important for people who are retiring to collect useful information and to make themselves known to people who may be able to influence any future work such as consultancy or to develop new roles and responsibilities.

Networking can be very useful in providing opportunities for paid and non-paid work. As we have read throughout this book many people do not want to stop work when they retire or they want to continue to make a professional contribution. Several colleagues, including Diana, Barbara and Jennifer, continue to work as governors. Others work in paid and non-paid work that provides stimulation and great satisfaction.

## Support at an organisational level

It is important for the institution to support all members of its workforce in their work-related transitions, and to benefit from the wisdom of its most experienced members. The health of an institution is indicated by how it treats its former employees and those who are making the transitions out of employment. I am proud of a recent initiative in our organisation. This is a staff development project involving or working with retired staff who in turn facilitate a number of learning activities. These are all aimed at recognising (and celebrating) the range of skills and knowledge that exist across the organisation. It means that we can avoid losing expertise when people retire, and it recognises that retirement does not mean having to stop contributing to the learning of others. The retirees include a dozen emeritus professors as well as other former employees and they support the following professional development activities:

- retiring workshops
- academic writing support
- writing workshops
- coaching and mentoring

- assisting with drafting research proposals
- work shadowing especially on international travels
- facilitating lunchtime or end-of-day workshops
- supporting staff with promotion application forms.

People's questions prompt me to consider whether 'retirement' is a useful word in this context. I looked at the *Concise Oxford Dictionary* and found the following definition of retirement: 'Seclusion, privacy, secluded place, a condition of having retired and receiving a pension (for having retired from) employment.' Such a definition sounds as if retired people need to be sent packing to a hideaway never to be seen again. I think not. My preferred view is that retiring is another professional or self-development journey. I believe that retirement in its broadest sense should not mean a complete separation from existing employers, unless that is the wish of the person, nor should it mean the end of paid employment. Flexible approaches need to be adopted so that organisations do not lose valuable people who have so much to offer and who want to continue to make a contribution.

My view is that the period that follows full- or part-time paid employment is a time when people should feel empowered. This is an opportunity to take control, make changes to life patterns, an opportunity to take bold steps, to experiment, a chance to take a few more risks, a time for lateral thinking.

I think that the prospect of retirement should be an opportunity to continue training, learning and development, just like any other working transition. I encourage those people who are approaching retirement to explore the following learning activities, at least several years before their official retirement.

## The activities

The second part of this chapter focuses on a number of activities related to the themes I have outlined above. The activities are designed to empower people, to help them take control, make changes to life patterns, encourage bold steps, help people experiment, to take a few more risks, and to support lateral thinking.

The following activities will be useful for people to engage in whether they are already retired or still have several years to go. Some of these suggestions will suit some better than others, especially as they overlap, emphasising different aspects of retiring.

### 1 Continuities and changes in retiring

*Purpose of the activity*: for many people the ideas of retiring are difficult to contemplate because they feel that everything will change. This activity is designed to help you consider what activities are important in your life before retirement, and which of these will continue afterwards, or to alert you so that you can plan to ensure they are still part of your life.

| Activity | | At present | In five years |
|---|---|---|---|
| Being creative | | | |
| Being intellectually challenged | | | |
| Going on holiday | | | |
| Going for lunch or a drink | | | |
| Getting financial advice | | | |
| Having a laugh | | | |
| Having a moan | | | |
| Taking exercise | | | |
| Planning for the future | | | |
| Sharing interests/hobbies | | | |
| Having a structured day | | | |
| Having a chat | | | |
| Taking care of someone | | | |
| Being taken care of | | | |
| Being comforted | | | |
| Being part of a family | | | |
| Discussing current events | | | |
| Discussing plans | | | |
| Staying healthy | | | |
| Ecological responsibility | | | |
| Emotional closeness | | | |
| Being respected | | | |
| Keeping up appearances | | | |
| [your choice of item] | | | |
| | | | |
| | | | |

(a) Decide which of these activities are important to you, or you would like to feature in your future life, using the empty column. You can of course add any that are not included.

(b) Make notes on what you do currently and what might be the same or different in the future. This might apply to the people you share these activities with, or other aspects of the activities.

(c) Reflect on what you noticed when you did this activity and what the implications are for you, if any.

## 2 Imagining a perfect retirement

*Purpose of this activity*: my advice would be 'Dare to dream'; by this I mean explore the life you want to live and live it. I know that retirement can be a bit scary as it may be a shift from your usual comfort zone, but change in retirement doesn't have to be that different from the present. It might only mean just a few tweaks.

This activity invites you to visualise your ideal situation, first in five years' time, and then at increasingly closer intervals. The importance lies in the details and specifics of your imagined future, your dream.

If you are working through this by yourself you may wish to make notes about your feelings and ideas at different stages of the activity (see table below). If you are in a group you may wish to discuss your feelings and ideas at different stages of the activity and perhaps to make notes as well.

(a) Think about yourself in five years' time and imagine yourself in the perfect or best possible situation:

- What are you doing?
- Who are you with?
- Where are you living?
- What are your surroundings like?
- What work, paid or unpaid, are you doing?
- What do you look like?
- How are you feeling?

(b) Now repeat these questions thinking of yourself in three years' time, then again in one years' time and then in six months' time.

(c) Now consider what you need to start doing in order to achieve or move towards your perfect situation. Draw up a list of the steps you need to take – now, in the next six months, in a year and so on. On the chart this means that you will work from the bottom up.

## A five-year plan

|  | The vision | Things to do to achieve the vision |
|---|---|---|
| Date in five years' time |  |  |
| Date in three years' time |  |  |
| Date in one years' time |  |  |
| Date in six months' time |  |  |

## 3 The importance of planning

*Purpose of this activity*: from the above exercises you will see that planning is crucial. My mantra is: if you fail to plan you plan to fail – while recognising an element of serendipity in all that we do and experience.

I believe that you need to treat your approach to retirement like a business opportunity and this needs a plan. This is a time for strategic thinking; you need to work out a timescale and start taking action now. Retiring as an aspect of professional development requires the individual to start planning early, develop strategies, revise the plan, and consult with others, perhaps a coach or a critical friend.

An action plan can be a very useful way of clarifying what you want to do and the steps you might take. Complete the following chart to help you with your plan.

| Long-term goal | Short-term and medium goals | Action | Constraints | Who or what can help me | Target for action |
|---|---|---|---|---|---|
|  |  |  |  |  |  |

### 4 Steps along the way

#### The wheel of life

*Purpose of this activity*: this is a useful exercise to identify areas of your life that you want to develop. Repeat it at intervals and observe how the pattern changes over time.

Draw a circle and divide it into eight segments, like slices of a cake. Label each segment with one of the eight most important aspects of your life. A fairly common combination would look something like this:

- health
- home
- finances
- fun and recreation
- partner and relationship
- friends and family
- work and career
- creativity and personal growth.

This is an illustrative combination, so feel free to adapt it to suit your current needs.

Now you need to assess (honestly and fairly!) how satisfied on a scale of 1 to 10 you are with each of these aspects in your life, perhaps keeping retiring in mind. As well as deciding an overall score, jot down the key factors that made you decide on that score.

Next, colour in each slice in proportion to its score. An aspect of your life scoring 10 would be all coloured in; one scoring 5 would be half-filled and one scoring 0 would not be coloured in at all. This gives you an immediate and powerful visual sense of how you are currently feeling about your life – both in your general sense of contentment and the balance between different aspects of your life. Reflect on the implications of this activity for retiring and for any changes you wish to make.

#### Taking stock

*Purpose of this activity*: the following questions invite you to consider some things you need to think about, and to make plans about. These may be to research or find out more about something (such as volunteering) or to check its availability or relevance to you (such as finances, or opportunities and resources available in your area). These questions should prompt you to take stock:

*Satisfactions in life and work*
- What aspects of your life (inside and outside work) provide the most satisfaction?
- What have been your top achievements over the last five years?
- What motivates you?
- Who have you enjoyed working with and why?
- How do people see you?

*Your skills*
- Skills that you want to use
- Skills that you would like to develop in your work
- Skills that you have but don't wish them to dominate in your work
- Skills that you have but don't want to use
- Transferable skills (knowledge, skills and understanding which could be used in other contexts)

*Your interests at work and during your leisure time*
- What would you like to spend more time doing?
- What interests do you pursue at the moment?
- What about evening classes?

*Your beliefs, values and guiding principles*
- What is important in your life that you wish to retain?
- What would constitute success for you?

*Your ambitions*
- Are you interested in promotion before retiring?
- Are your ambitions for retiring similar to your ambitions in your working life or are you interested in a completely different post/role?

*Consider your constraints*
- Do you have care of parents, children, grandchildren, location, partner or other…?
- Are you likely to acquire or lose any caring relationships in the future?

*Consider your time*
- How many hours/days a week do you want to work in the immediate future?
- How many hours/days a week do you want to work prior to retirement?
- How many hours/days a week do you want to work when you have retired?

*Consider you finances*
- How much money do you need/want to earn before you retire?
- How much money do you need to earn/want following retiring?
- Would volunteering be appropriate?

*If you are considering a new direction what could it look like?*
- Face up to the question: What if …?
- What is stopping you doing what you want to do now? (Recognising that what often stops us doing what we want to do is ourselves.)
- Change your mindset to seeing retirement as having the power to create a positive living environment for yourself.
- Finding oneself from within.

## 5 Getting support

### Communities

*Purpose of this activity:* many people find that they fear the loss of human contact when they retire. This activity encourages you to think about what you can do to maintain your 'communities' and to build some more.

It has been suggested that everybody needs a minimum of three communities to lead a healthy life. The communities are groups of people who have contact with each other. Most people have one based on their family and loved ones. Work often provides a second community. It is the loss of this community that people may fear will leave a large gap. Your third community may come from any number of groups, and these may be connected in a range of ways: formal, closely or loosely connected, virtual, interest-based and so on.

Here is a list provided in a few minutes by a group of seven people considering retiring:

| Family and loved ones | Work | Local church |
|---|---|---|
| Singing and choir | School pals | London bat group |
| Reading group | Allotments association | Lace making |
| Trade union | Adult education | Walking |
| Stitching group | Volunteering | Holiday friends |
| Democrats abroad | Theatre-going | email group |
| Anorexia support group | Concert-going | Ballet-going |
| Tai Chi | Art circle | Activities with partner |

You can see that the communities in this group often have a shared activity or focus which gives them purpose, and that they range from formal membership to very loose connections. They may meet weekly, less frequently or only through the Internet. But they all provide human contact.

Make your own list of communities of which you are presently a member, not forgetting your family and work communities. Consider what will happen to these communities over the next five years, which are likely to continue and which will no longer remain. Consider also the range of communities and whether you would like to add different kinds of communities. Then you can plan to build up new connections, perhaps changing some of the work connections.

### Find yourself a coach, mentor or counsellor

Join or set up a pre-retirement group to share thoughts, hopes and dreams (see Chapters 2 and 3).

### 6 Networking: how to use formal and informal networks and organisations

I think the benefits of networking are:
- to collect useful information
- to make yourself known to people who may be able to influence any future work/consultancy/role.

*Purpose of the activity*: the following activity will help you consider how to network effectively and how to generate contacts.

*Developing a strategy:*
- decide what you want to achieve
- identify the most appropriate contact
- consider how you might impress them. Find out as much as possible about the people and the role that you might want beforehand. This will avoid time-wasting – yours and theirs. Even if you are only gathering information at this stage, it might be worth having a targeted CV to hand just in case the person you are talking to asks to see it. They might be able to suggest some improvements.

Think about generating contacts through:
- – people you already know
- – people you almost know, friend of a friend
- – complete strangers – generated through professional agencies, trade directories or lists of university alumni.

Think about how you might approach contacts:
- how do you first approach a contact; what is the most appropriate way (for example, a telephone call, email or letter)
- you may need to chase with a gentle reminder.

Think about meetings:
- try to generate at least two contacts from every meeting you attend
- know when to leave, keep an eye on body language
- keep records of every meeting and all your contacts
- send thank you letters or emails.

### 7  The opportunities for paid and non-paid work: consultancy, working from home, volunteering

*The purpose of this activity:* many people do not want to stop work or making a professional contribution when they are retiring. In this section you will be invited to consider what you could offer if you want to go on using your skills.

(a)  Complete a SWOT analysis.
The SWOT analysis will help you identify your:

Strengths, Weaknesses, Opportunities, Threats.

Use the table to note all your ideas – be imaginative and put the ideas down in any order:

| *Strengths* | *Weaknesses* |
|---|---|
| *Opportunities* | *Threats* |

(b)  After completing your SWOT analysis you should ask yourself:

- How can I use my strengths to enable me to take advantage of the opportunities I have identified?
- How can I use these strengths to overcome the threats identified?

- How do I overcome the identified weaknesses in order to take advantage of the opportunities?
- How will I minimise my weaknesses to overcome the identified threats?

The SWOT analysis aims to help you choose the most suitable action and to make the most of your choices. Predicting threats can help you make decisions about what to do before they happen, enabling you to be proactive rather than reactive.

(c) Think about a possible action plan. What would it look like? Who might you approach for help? What timescale are you working to? How would you know when you have achieved each stage of your action plan?

## 8 Some final dos and don'ts

- Do look for opportunities to develop new skills, interests and new learning
- Don't underestimate the extensive body of skills that you already possess
- Do use networking strategies to research your job options
- Don't restrict your job search to your current field; your knowledge and skills will be in demand elsewhere
- Do keep updating your CV.

Whatever your objectives and reasons, make sure they are your own and not what you think your partner, your manager, your family and friends, or organisation wants you to do.

# Chapter 17

# Helping people to the other side: recurring themes from a financial adviser

## Sid Reddy

*'The question isn't at what age I want to retire, it's at what income.'*

George Foreman

The editors asked Sid Reddy to identify the major themes he found when helping people think about financial aspects of retiring. In his own phrase, he has helped many of the contributors in this book 'to the other side'. We wanted to draw on his considerable expertise in helping people think about how financial planning can help realise people's hopes for retiring for the readers of this book.

I work as an independent financial adviser and have known many of the contributors in this book for close to 15 years. I have (modestly) helped them with their planning towards retirement and also seen them safely to the other side! I have always considered my contribution to be to take money worries out of the retirement equation. I do this because money really is only one part of retiring and there are a lot of other factors to be considered (which have been covered by the other contributors).

Much of what I say below has come about from conversations with many people who have retired and, hopefully, is of help to those planning how they retire.

## Pension tension

It is common nowadays to reach retirement age having worked for many different employers and included breaks for many reasons. It is also common for pension schemes to be of different types and this is probably why many I see dread to even open any correspondence to do with pensions.

Put simply, very simply, there are two different types of pension schemes. The first one is where your employer guarantees your pension based only on the number of years of loyal service. These are called defined benefit schemes because, as the name suggests, the benefits you get are defined. If you are in one of these schemes, it truly is a reason to celebrate.

The second type is where the benefits you get depend on contributions made by you and your employer and on how these contributions grow over time, linked to the stock markets. If the stock markets do well, your pension will be larger and should convert into a bigger pension. However, what you get back also depends on the annuity rate that is used to calculate your benefits. With this kind of pension, timing is everything. It is, therefore, important to see your financial adviser more frequently.

## When to consult your financial adviser about retirement

I am always being asked when is the best time to start talking seriously about retiring. My answer is that it is at about the time you actually start to open any correspondence about retirement from your employer or pension provider rather than neatly piling it on your desk! The correct answer? The sooner the better.

You should be consulting financial advisers right through your working career about various aspects of financial planning, tedious as these discussions tend to be! If you are thinking about retiring at age 60 (say), you should start serious conversations with your financial adviser at the age of 50 or so. This gives you ten years when your earning power is at its maximum to do what you can towards your pension.

This also gets your mind ticking about what it is you will be doing in retirement and how your retirement would affect loved ones such as partners, children and elderly relatives. It starts conversations about changes such as selling properties and making the most of existing savings and investments.

I find that, at about age 55, people start to show real interest in what I am telling them about their retirement income. This is because, as one of them said, retirement becomes a real possibility! Imagine having to wait to talk about life insurance until death became a real possibility!

## When will you retire and what will you get?

Now that we are all living much longer because of medical advancements, your 'longest holiday' needs to be better planned. Ideally, you need a financial adviser who can put things simply. Talk to friends and colleagues if you do not already have a financial adviser you can trust. I tend to sit down with clients three years before their proposed retirement date and work out what I call 'net monthly income'.

This is money that you will be able to touch, feel and spend, having paid all taxes. It is important to know this figure as you approach retirement. It is important that you ask your financial adviser to work this figure out based on pessimistic growth projections. You will want to have a 'worst case scenario net monthly income' figure. You may be getting £2,000 (say) in to your bank account each month in employment and your financial adviser works out that you will have £1,500 every month in retirement. The difference between the two figures may not be as dire as it seems. You will need to calculate your work-related expenses and any money you save on a monthly figure. That will then give you your first glimpse into financial life in retirement.

It is important to recalculate the net monthly income figure every few months as you approach retirement to reflect any changes in salary and the value of investments and pension funds.

You need to then agree on a plan to pay off any debts you have, including mortgages, car loans and such like. You may plan to use a lump sum that you get from your employer on retirement to do this. Your plan might be to just sell what you have got and downsize or move out of the area you are in.

Discuss any investments in detail with your financial adviser and agree how much risk (if any) you are prepared to take for growth on investments. Ideally, you need to reduce your aversion to risk in retirement and it is best to have this conversation with your financial adviser.

Apart from attitude to risk, get an explanation as to how much access you would have to your investments and whether it would cost any money. It is best to have access to a pot of money so you need not panic if any emergency situations turn up. At the risk of boring you, I will repeat myself: it is best to have access to a pot of money so you need not panic if any emergency situations turn up.

## Where would you live and what would it cost?

You were probably influenced by proximity to or easy travel to and from work when you purchased the property in which you now live. In retirement, happily, you are free from such influences! Some people decide to sell their property and move out of the cities in retirement. My advice has always been to consider renting for a while unless you already really know the area where you want to move. Other influences will become more important in your choice of where to buy. Apart from the usual ones to do with family, friends and access to shops, an important factor should be to do with access to, and cost of, quality health and dental care.

You should talk with your financial adviser about how to invest any excess monies not spent on the purchase of your property.

## Living abroad

Increasingly, people are retiring to sunnier climes all over the world to enjoy their 'life-long holiday'. My advice, as you might guess, is to rent for a while in the area in which you intend to buy. This will give you a test run before committing to buying your house in the sun. Where you buy and what you buy will depend largely on your personal preferences. Apart from considering number of hours of sunshine during the day and quality of local wines in the evening, your decisions will now be influenced by exchange rates and how far your British Pound will stretch locally. Access to, and cost of, local health and dental care should also be an important consideration. There might be medical insurance policies available locally and it is vital to understand the specifics of what they cover. There might be perfectly adequate, and free, access to local medical care. You will need to establish this by talking with other retirees in the area and getting them to recount their experiences over a glass or two of local wine! Keep in mind that you may have lost access to NHS services in the UK by moving abroad.

If you decide to retire abroad, you may require your income in the local currency. Most pension providers will, for a cost, agree to send you your pension income into your local bank account. Your financial adviser should be able to do the same for any income from investments. You may want to talk to your financial adviser about the practicality of investing in your new currency. If your income is in Pounds and the Pounds are buying fewer Euros (say), this directly affects your lifestyle.

Property taxes also vary from place to place as do laws to do with succession (inheritance). It is best to have a serious talk with your solicitor before your purchase of the property. Keep in mind that while you are expressing yourself in English at 100 mph, your local contact, whose first language may not be English, is only taking in what you say at 10 mph!

If you decide to move abroad permanently, your financial adviser will talk to you about off-shore investments and such like so that your investments are arranged in the most tax-efficient manner.

## I just don't know if I am ready to retire yet!

It is entirely normal to have doubts about the decision to retire. This is perhaps because you cannot ever be entirely sure if everything will be as rosy as others say. Some employers now allow employees to take part-time retirement. Basically, you start to draw down on your retirement benefits and continue to be employed for a part of the time. This will give you the chance to test-drive retirement before taking the plunge. It might be a good idea to talk with your employer and see if they would offer you that option.

## Is the future really rosy?

Yes. Money rarely becomes an issue in retirement and this is because you get used to what income you are on very quickly and cut your cloth accordingly.

## Staying in touch

With mobiles, BlackBerries and broadband, staying in touch has never been easier. You will want to give up on getting instant responses to calls and emails as you should be more relaxed and separated from the workplace that required instant action on everything. I encourage you to have Internet access to your investments if you want to keep an eye on things in retirement. You should still talk to your financial adviser once or twice a year just to make sure that your investments are on track and that you are aware of any changes in tax legislation.

# Chapter 18

# Reasons to be cheerful

Eileen Carnell, Marianne Coleman,
Jennifer Evans, Anne Gold, Alison Kirton,
Diana Leonard, Caroline Lodge, Anne Peters

*'You are only young once, but you can stay immature indefinitely.'*

Anon.

> This chapter discusses many things to look forward to when retiring. The chapter is written by the eight members of the Retiring Women group who outline the benefits of retiring under three main categories: the sense of freedom that retiring brings, the financial gains for people over a certain age, and the joys of becoming older and wiser.

## Introduction

During our third residential weekend in May 2008, the Retiring Women group members all worked together to generate ideas about what we experience as the benefits of retiring. We all wanted to contribute to this chapter. We came up with the title that we love: reasons to be cheerful. The purpose of this chapter is to pass on to other retirees what we think there is to look forward to when retiring.

While we are all mindful of the view that for some of these benefits there may be downsides, we want to focus on the advantage of retiring and end the book on a high note.

We are aware of the potential changes in the political climate and some of these benefits may alter over the next few years. We are also aware of different contexts. The Retiring Women group members live in London mostly and benefits in different parts of the country and world may be different. Another consideration is that this chapter is written from the perspective of women – and men may have different gains.

After sharing our ideas in the group we analysed the list under three main headings:

- the sense of freedom that retiring brings;
- the financial gains for people over a certain age; and
- the joys of becoming older and wiser.

While we are aware that these three areas are inextricably linked we now consider each in turn.

## Reasons to be cheerful – part 1: freedom

It is not surprising that the majority of ideas generated by the Retiring Women group fall into this category. We feel that not having to commit to a regular work pattern for the days, weeks and years of retiring, compared to possibly 40 years of work, provides a sense of freedom. Added to which there is a freedom from career planning.

The ideas cover some very practical points. We start with those which include how people see their days differently:

- being able to wake up naturally in the morning
- having time to read the newspaper
- being able to read novels during daylight hours
- joining daytime classes for pleasurable activities, including specific over sixties events.

The group members are also mindful of other areas of freedom that retiring brings and the fact that there is less pressure on us to conform to other people's demands:

- being able to plan trips away outside school holidays (especially for teachers)
- enjoying long weekends and mid-week breaks (which may be available at short notice).

We notice a different attitude to time: time belongs to us. There is time to:

- be spontaneous
- talk without having to rush off to another appointment

- have long lunches with friends
- resuscitate friendships and enjoy friendships that are long-standing
- think and make decisions
- make ourselves more comfortable in our homes and to de-clutter – life laundry
- rearrange and appreciate our treasured possessions
- do what we want to do now
- spend with family and feel freer in everything we do
- do voluntary work
- do all the things we have been putting off
- think and be in the moment
- babysit, care for younger and older members of the family and support friends
- take long walks and/or walk the dog
- keep fit and prepare and experiment with lovely food
- look for sale bargains
- reflect on our good and lovely memories.

## Reasons to be cheerful – part 2: financial gains

One important area of discussion in the Retiring Women group is that most of us have time and money at the same time for the first time in our lives. Most of us feel that we are in a good position in that we are not worried about money and that we have the time to enjoy the pleasures that the combination of time and money can bring.

First we talked about all the regular financial benefits and allowances retiring brings:

- receiving an occupational pension (for us we are able to claim this at 60; it varies with date of birth and gender)
- receiving a state pension (for us we are also able to claim this at 60; it varies with date of birth and gender too)
- not having to pay National Insurance at 60 (this may vary with date of birth and gender)
- receiving the annual winter fuel allowance (again this may change in the future) and when we get older the TV licence is waived and there may be other age-related benefits
- enjoying the benefits of the Freedom Pass which now includes travel across the country on buses and on the Tube in London for free.

There are also free eye tests, hearing tests and prescriptions for medicines.

Other financial benefits are available that may be dependent on local authorities. We find it is worth researching what is available in one's local area. For example, many of us benefit from:

- reduced fees for day and evening classes, keep fit, gym, other exercises classes and free swimming and water aerobics classes
- facilities available for people over a certain age – e.g. lunchtime clubs, walking groups.

We all enjoy getting money off for some activities, when shopping and travelling. For example:

- theatre and cinemas may offer discounts on certain days of the week and for certain performances
- many shops have discount cards. DIY chains have particular days of the week when they offer discounts to people over a certain age
- chains of chemists have over-sixties cards so that all their own products have a 10 per cent discount
- senior rail cards can be bought which allow people to have greatly reduced rail fares.

It is worth checking with shops. For example, some hardware stores offer discounts and some cafes and pubs have reduced prices on some days, especially at lunchtimes.

The general opinion of the Retiring Women group is that we have worked hard for so long, we have paid our dues and we have earned what we are entitled to – so enjoy!

### Reasons to be cheerful – part 3: the joys of becoming older and wiser

Our third set of reasons to be cheerful is more difficult to define. These seem to be about the fact that we are getting older. Perhaps this is why they seemed to generate more controversy in our discussion and there is more ambiguity around them.

The most positive aspect of becoming older is to do with wisdom. Several of us in the group talked about:

- recognising that you know a lot and for this reason get respect from others
- being able to express oneself confidently
- having a carefully considered opinion
- being able to draw on a wealth of experience to inform an argument
- being able to use our skills and experience in non-work situations

- feeling that people want to listen and talk to us and maybe ask for our advice
- realising better what is important and being able to distinguish between what is worth worrying about and what is worth letting go.

Finally we discussed the benefits in becoming older and the confidence that we often feel about not needing to be so sensible and the excitement of being able to try new things for the first time – including some of the following, although some of us have tried a few of these things already:

**Warning**
by Jenny Joseph

*When I am an old woman I shall wear purple*
*With a red hat which doesn't go, and doesn't suit me.*
*And I shall spend my pension on brandy and summer gloves*
*And satin sandals, and say we've no money for butter.*
*I shall sit down on the pavement when I'm tired*
*And gobble up samples in shops and press alarm bells*
*And run my stick along the public railings*
*And make up for the sobriety of my youth.*
*I shall go out in my slippers in the rain*
*And pick the flowers in other people's gardens*
*And learn to spit.*

*You can wear terrible shirts and grow more fat*
*And eat three pounds of sausages at a go*
*Or only bread and pickle for a week*
*And hoard pens and pencils and beermats and things in boxes.*

*But now we must have clothes that keep us dry*
*And pay our rent and not swear in the street*
*And set a good example for the children.*
*We must have friends to dinner and read the papers.*

*But maybe I ought to practise a little now?*
*So people who know me are not too shocked and surprised*
*When suddenly I am old, and start to wear purple.*

Reprinted from *Selected Poems*, Bloodaxe 1992.
Reproduced with permission of Johnson & Alcock Ltd.

## Closing thoughts

This chapter considers many of the reasons to be cheerful in the freedom that retiring brings, the financial gains and the advantages of becoming older and wiser. But as we read across the chapters in the book there are other far more important issues in making our retiring lives fulfilling and happy. The narratives tell of the struggles in the transitions that people face and in the struggles in finding new identities. Becoming 'retired' is a long process that is often challenging, hard work and problematic. Periods of depression, loneliness and physical illness are discussed. What we find as we read these retiring stories is a high level of courage, creativity and generosity and hope that people use them to find satisfaction, meaning, point and purpose in their lives. The experiments that people make often add richness to their lives and to the lives of others that is way beyond the reasons to be cheerful. We conclude that from the stories we read in this book it is our relationships with others that is most important. It is the opportunity to develop further our closeness with our families, friends and loved ones that is the gift of retiring.

# Appendix: bibliography and contacts

Eileen Carnell, Marianne Coleman,
Jennifer Evans, Anne Gold, Alison Kirton,
Diana Leonard, Caroline Lodge, Anne Peters

This Appendix provides an annotated bibliography of some of the books and other forms of information that we have found helpful in thinking about retiring and how we want to live our lives. It is a fairly random collection including fiction and non-fiction. We have divided the Appendix into several sections: novels; poetry collections; transitions, retiring information and older lives; health and bereavement. We end with three lists: interesting biographies/autobiographies; relevant films and some useful contacts.

1 Novels
2 Poetry collections
3 Transitions, retiring information and older lives
4 Health and bereavement
5 Biographies and autobiographies
6 Films on the theme of ageing
7 Useful contacts

## 1 Novels

**Elizabeth Buchan (2002)** *Revenge of the Middle-Aged Woman.* **Penguin.**

I don't think I will read the companion volume (*The Second Wife*) mostly because I disliked the character in this book, and have little sympathy with her. The story concerns a woman who is dumped by her husband for her younger friend, and this woman takes her job and her home too. The revenge is that the first wife (Rose) makes a better life for herself than her erring husband and friend. This is done quite subtly, and over time. The hurt and pain of the early betrayal is well drawn, but so is Rose's realisation that she had the best years with her husband, and neither that life, nor her two children can be taken from her. We leave her about to rekindle her first love.

The story is told from the position of the first wife. The narrative includes many flashbacks. It's told in a somewhat jaunty style, very readable, something of a page-turner. Slight but enjoyable (CL).

**Terry Darlington (2005)** *Narrow Dog to Carcassonne.* **Bantam Press.**

This story begins when Terry and Monica retire and decide to sail their narrow-boat across the channel and down to the Mediterranean. The best part of the story I think is how their Whippet Jim reacts to this death-defying adventure. It is a funny and beautifully written book and will delight anyone who is interested in narrow-boats, dogs or France or none of these things but just enjoys a good tale (EC).

**Margaret Forster (1989)** *Have the Men had Enough?* **Chatto & Windus.**

I read this when it first came out to try and understand dementia – a condition my mother had for many years. I would recommend it to anyone who has a family member or friend with this condition. It focuses on a grandmother's descent into dementia with remarkable insight and the effects on the different members of her family. It is sad but very funny in places and well worth reading (EC).

**Jane Gardam (2004)** *Old Filth.* **Chatto & Windus.**

This is a wonderfully written book and is, in effect, the life story of a man who became a lawyer and then a judge in Hong Kong (Filth jokingly stands for Failed in London, Try Hong Kong). The book is set at the end of his life when he is old, widowed and has retired to Dorset. It is only at the end of his life that he can look back and come to a better understanding of many of the events that he recalls (MC).

**Mark Haddon (2007)** *A Spot of Bother.* **Vintage.**

I read this because it was supposed to be about retiring. But actually it isn't. The main character is having a serious breakdown because he refuses to face up to so much in his life: his wife's affair, his son's and daughter's adult problems, the possibility of ill-health and above all death. Each of the characters in his life has a very clear way of coping, which all falls apart as George does.

It is written to amuse, and some of the set pieces are funny – especially when George is doing something quite bonkers, but which he sees as just the best thing to do: lying in the ditch on his daughter's wedding day, taking lots of Valium, getting drunk, ignoring the vision of his wife in flagrante delicto, and clocking his wife's lover one at the wedding.

In the end the power of love, of friendship and of mutuality is what Haddon seems to be preaching. It's amusing, but not great fiction (CL).

**Virginia Ironside (2006)** *No! I Don't Want to Join a Bookclub.* **Penguin.**

Nice easy read. I have described it in an offer to pass it on to the Retiring Women group as Chick Lit meets Grumpy Old Woman. Rather satisfying read as it turns out that our heroine is heading for a relationship with a very old friend called Archie (CL).

**Doris Lessing (1997)** *Love, Again.* **Flamingo.**

This is the story of Sarah Durham, a 60-year-old producer and founder of a fringe theatre. During the commissioning and setting up of a new play, she meets and unexpectedly falls in love with two younger men – one after the other, causing her to relive her own stages of growing up, from 'crushes' to mature and lasting attachments. Love also brings the desolation of loss (CL).

> *To fall in love is to remember one is an exile, and that is why the sufferer does not want to be cured, even while crying, 'I can't endure this non-life, I can't endure this desert'.*

**Doris Lessing (1973)** *The Summer Before the Dark.* **Alfred A. Knopf.**

Published in 1973, this is very much of its time. It reveals the life of Kate Brown, an able, intelligent and attractive woman, now middle-aged, who has been 'just' a housewife and mother. Her abilities, which have been underestimated by her family and those who know her, are revealed when she gets drawn into the world of 'Global Food' and international conferences. The book is about transformations in different contexts. But the particular transformation that has stayed in the memory of three of us in the Retiring Women group was the extraordinary moment when she realises how easy it is for a middle-aged or older woman to become virtually invisible.

Kate is watching men working on a building when she realises that they are taking no notice of her:

> *The fact that they didn't suddenly made her angry. She walked away out of sight, and there, took off her jacket – Maureen's – showing her fitting dark dress. She strolled back in front of the workmen, hips conscious of themselves. A storm of whistles, calls, invitations. Out of sight the other way, she made her small transformation and walked back again: the men glanced at her, did not see her. She was trembling with rage: it was a rage, it seemed to her, that she had been suppressing for a lifetime.*

Although she interprets this revelation as undermining her past life, the understanding also gives her power. Her mature attractiveness is shown to be skin deep but her transformations through the summer including her rebirth as a career woman have brought her greater self-knowledge. We liked that (MC).

**David Lodge (2008)** *Deaf Sentence.* **Harvill Secker.**

This is a tale of a recently retired professor whose younger wife is going up in her career as he floats down in his. It contains the usual David Lodge blend of laugh-out-loud scenes (a family Christmas; interactions – they can barely be called conversations – with the narrator's father who is even more deaf that he is; a foreign research student who uses sexual and intellectual wiles to try to get staff to write her PhD for her; and lip-reading classes, among others) and really interesting insights into the experience of being 'hard of hearing' or 'hearing impaired' or, 'not to put too fine a point on it, deaf – not profoundly deaf, but deaf enough to make communication imperfect in most social situations and impossible in some'. It also teaches us, in Lodge's wonderful applied linguist's way, why, for instance, consonants cause the deaf particular problems, and why 'deafness is comic, as blindness is tragic' (DL).

> *Consonants are voiced at higher frequency than vowels. I could hear vowels perfectly well – still can. But it's consonants that we mainly depend on to distinguish one word from another. '"Did you say pig or fig?" said the Cat. "I said pig", replied Alice.' Maybe the Cheshire Cat was a bit deaf: it wasn't sure whether Alice had used a bi-labial plosive or a labiodental frictive the first time she pronounced the word.*
> *(p. 19)*

**Barbara Pym (1977, reissued 2004)** *Quartet in Autumn.* **Pan.**

This tale remains rather sad until nearly the last chapter. Four people work together in an office, doing unspecified work. The two men and two women are all single (although they have not all been single all their lives). Their lives have little in them, although each has made a small effort to do something, whether it is to engage with the church, admire her surgeon and collect milk bottles, be bitter or plan for retirement in the country.

The women retire, and the death of one of them brings the others together in a strange way, but one that in the end speaks of the individual's ability to make choices and influence others. 'But at least it made one realise that life still held infinite possibilities for change', the novel concludes. On the way to this conclusion, every tiny action or event is squeezed by the quartet for its meaning and engagement (CL).

**Bernice Rubens (1990)** *The Five-year Sentence.* **Abacus Books.**

I read this book years ago, long before I began to think about retiring and it is one of those rare books that I read three or four times. It is a grim but gripping tale of a woman who is planning suicide rather than face the prospect of a lonely and miserable retirement. Used to obeying orders all her life she is faced with a leaving present of a five-year diary and this forces her to make a diary entry every day. The first entries are boring instructions but gradually become more bizarre and outrageous. The book conjures up a very lonely existence and desperation but it is witty and darkly humorous (EC).

**Salley Vickers (2000)** *Miss Garnet's Angel.* **HarperCollins.**

Following the unexpected death of her friend, Miss Garnet, a retired history teacher and ex-Communist party member, rents an apartment in Venice for the winter. I loved the sensitive way that the novel charts the adventures and misadventures of a woman alone, against the rich backdrop of the art, architecture and religious history of Venice. The story of Tobias and the Angel is told in parallel as a device to bring together the complex elements of Julia Garnet's contemporary journey. Such a journey involves an examination of love, death, sexuality and religious values in an intriguing and delightful way. For those of us in the *troisième âge*, this is an honest and inspiring multilayered account of the possibilities that a spell of retirement in a foreign city can bring (AK).

## 2 Poetry collections

*Soul Food; Nourishing Poems for Starved Minds*, edited by Neil Astley and Pamela Roberson-Pearce and published by Bloodaxe (2007). A kind of cheesy title but, like all the anthologies I've got from Bloodaxe, a really interesting collection of poems (AP).

*Penguin's Poems for Life*, selected by Laura Barber and published by Penguin Classics (2007). It sort of goes through the life cycle and has sections headed 'Getting Older, Looking Back' – 'Intimations of Mortality' – 'Mourning and Monuments'. Cheery isn't it? But the poems selected are good (AP).

*Staying Alive; Real Poems for Unreal Times*, edited by Neil Astley and published by Bloodaxe (2004). I think this is a wonderful anthology. And it has an excellent follow-up in …

*Being Alive*, again Neil Astley and Bloodaxe (2004) – which is a sequel in the same spirit.

*52 Ways of Looking at a Poem*, by Ruth Padel and published by Vintage (2004). She gives you 52 poems, each with short (one to two pages) commentary which really expands the way I read and understood the poems. Wonderful. She is a poet herself and a fantastic speaker. These come from a column she did, I now learn, in *The Independent*. Fantastic (AP).

*The Poem and the Journey; 60 Poems for the Journey of Life*, by Ruth Padel published by Chatto & Windus/Random House (2007). This is her new book on poetry and also wonderful (AP).

*Ten Poems to Change Your Life*, by Roger Housden published by Hodder & Stoughton (2001). As Caroline said – totally horrible if you are reading him (complete opposite of Ruth Padel) but the selection is good (AP).

And a single poem:

'*Warning*' by Jenny Joseph, published in SELECTED POEMS, Bloodaxe 1992.

## 3 Transitions, retiring information and older lives

**Mary Ann Anderson (2007) 'The aging experience'. Chapter 2 in *Caring for Older Adults Holistically*. F.A. Davis Company.**

This was a really good find in my local library. Yes, it is American and yes, it is written for nurses and health workers but I found this chapter to be the most comprehensive and holistic account of the ageing process. It takes a critical look at ageism, discusses six common theories of ageing and examines age-related changes in all the body systems. Other chapters include 'Promoting wellness', 'Nutrition' and 'End-of-life issues' (EC).

**Diana Athill (2008) *Somewhere Towards the End*. Granta.**

Something akin to a memoir or essays, but more a sort of conversation about old age and what having had an interesting life means for old age (CL).

> *There are no lessons to be learnt, no discoveries to be made, no solutions to offer. I find myself left with nothing but a few random thoughts. One of them is that from up here I can look back and see that although human life is less than a blink of an eyelid in terms of the universe, within its own framework it is amazingly capacious so that it can contain many opposites. One life can hold serenity and tumult, heartbreak and happiness, coldness and warmth, grabbing and giving – and also more particular opposites such as a neurotic conviction that one is a flop and a consciousness of success amounting to smugness.... So an individual life is interesting enough to merit examination.... What dies is not a life's value, but the worn out (or damaged) container of the self, together with the self's awareness of itself: away that goes into nothingness, with everyone else's. (pp. 177–81)*

**Rosemary Brown (1995)** *Good Non-retirement Guide.* **Kogan Page.**

This is a comprehensive book covering the range of subjects one might expect and would be useful for people who want an overview of these issues: looking forward to retirement including pre-retirement courses; money in general; pensions; tax; investment; financial advisers; budget planner; your home; leisure activities; looking for paid work; voluntary work; health; holidays; caring for elderly parents; no one is immortal! We wrote our book as an antidote to this approach to retirement, but this guide is useful for very practical issues (EC).

**John Burningham (2002)** *The Time of Your Life.* **Bloomsbury.**

This miscellany of ponderings and illustrations portrays the wisdom and wit that comes with age. I particularly liked Mary Wesley's two-page reflections on getting older, Winston Churchill's paragraph on painting, a delightful piece by Alec Guinness on his experience with a new mobile phone and the one-liners:

- 'Old age isn't so bad when you consider the alternative' (Maurice Chevalier on his seventy-second birthday, 9 October 1960, *New York Times*)
- 'If I'd known I was gonna live this long, I'd have taken better care of myself' (Eubie Blake, jazz musician, 13 February 1983, *The Observer*, Sayings of the Week).

A good book for the loo (EC).

**Jane Fearnley-Whittingstall (2005)** *The Good Granny Guide: Or how to be a modern grandmother.* **Short Books.**

Practical and down-to-earth advice with a light touch, for grannies (and grandfathers) who want to be involved in the upbringing of their offspring's offspring. The advice is along the lines of: be there for them all, don't offer advice unless requested and provide relief for the parents. The author also includes many practical ideas about entertaining grandchildren, including invaluable advice to practise assembling buggies, car seats and prams in advance (CL).

**Liz Ford (2007)** *The Guardian Guide to Volunteering.* **Guardian Newspapers.**

When I retired I got a copy of this from my local library and read it from cover to cover, imagining all the different sorts of voluntary work I could do. It is an excellent resource for anyone looking for something fascinating and worthwhile to do when they have finished paid work. It is fully comprehensive, covering relevant contacts for: Working with children and young people, Animals and wildlife, Environment and conservation, People with disabilities/health, Elderly people, Prisoners and ex-offenders, Homelessness, Refugees, Sports, and Going overseas (EC).

This could be read alongside an investigation of the charity Reach which helps experienced people match their skills to the needs of voluntary organisations:

http://www.reach-online.org.uk/

**Barbara Macdonald with Cynthia Rich (1984)** *Look Me in the Eye: Old women, aging and ageism.* **Spinsters Ink Books.**

One I have had on my bookshelf a very long time but recently reread. Barbara Macdonald, Cynthia Rich and others consider their own and others' attitudes towards older women. Each of the essays discusses the lives of older women and takes up issues we have been talking about in our Retiring Women group, such as being invisible, being judged because of our grey hair and ageing skin, and not being considered to be contributing members of society (EC).

**Debbie Rowe and Tracey Larcombe (2007)** *50 over 50: Extraordinary women, extraordinary lives.* **Dewi Lewis Media Ltd.**

The back cover of this book suggests that '50 over 50 is an inspirational and life-affirming book, which will stir the imaginations of women about to turn 50, as well as those who are already there and beyond'. I think it does just that. It is a lovely book and I love the portraits of the women as much as the interviews. The 50 women are depicted as being powerful and in control of their lives. This book was sponsored by Dove as part of the Dove ProAge campaign which was based on research which highlighted common misconceptions held about older women. The research illustrated the need for media to do a better job portraying realistic yet inspirational women. So the portraits in this book contrast with the images so often portrayed of older women.

The interviews include those you would expect such as Baroness Valerie Amos, Lynda La Plante, Doreen Lawrence, Zandra Rhodes and those I have never heard of before such as Linda de Cossart, a consultant vascular and general surgeon, Thope Lekau who runs a B&B in the Kaleisha Township in South Africa, Elizabeth Schofield who learned to read and write at 76 years old and Ordell Safran, a llama farmer.

The short interviews are a good read. When I first bought the book I read one story a day. Now I often look at the portraits and dip into the text. The two authors worked their way round the world to interview women and now donate from the royalties to ActionAid (EC).

**Susan Hemmings (1985)** *A Wealth of Experience: The lives of older women.* **Pandora Press.**

Another set of essays that I reread when I was writing my chapter for this book. I found it very useful and inspiring. I was moved by some of the stories and helped, in particular, by those that looked at the transitions of retiring. It is a book of its time and it is interesting to compare the difference in experiences contained in the narratives here in this book, written 23 years later (EC).

**Gail Sheehy (1997)** *New Passages: Managing your life across time.* **HarperCollins.**

This is in the style of many US self-help texts, but considers changes from middle life on in a way that some people will find helpful. There is a UK edition (CL).

## 4 Health and bereavement

**Elizabeth Arden, Nigel Arden and David Hunter (2008)** *Osteoarthritis.* **Oxford University Press.**

I loved this little book. It is packed with useful information, diagrams and helpful hints. For anyone with aching joints and painful knees, as I have, it will be most helpful. The layout is really good, the key points, bullet point lists and question-and-answer sections are useful and the whole book is easy to read and well researched. I came away feeling a lot more knowledgeable and thinking that I could take some positive action (EC).

**BBC (Foreword by Esther Rantzen) (2006)** *How to Have a Good Death: Preparing and planning with informed choices and practical advice.* **Dorling Kindersley.**

A wonderfully straightforward and really useful book. It covers a number of helpful and explicit areas that make thinking, planning and talking about death normal and explicit: How do people die; Communication and coping emotionally; Caring for someone who is dying; Bereavement and mourning; Funerals and memorial services; Planning your death (EC).

**Joan Didion (2006)** *The Year of Magical Thinking.* **Harper's Perennial.**

A very personal and revealing account of grief, the year in question being the year when Joan Didion waited for her husband to return. She knew he was dead, but she believed that he could come back to her, so she should not give away his shoes, end some thought patterns, stop some old habits. It's about living in a world where everything has changed, and suddenly, and the relationship to everything changes because you are no longer sharing a life. I read it very quickly, but couldn't stop reading it (CL).

**Germaine Greer (1991)** *The Change: Women, ageing, and the menopause.* **Ballantine Books.**

The *New York Times* called this book a 'brilliant, gutsy, exhilarating, exasperating fury of a book'. It became an influential book in the women's movement. In it, Greer wrote of the various myths concerning menopause, advising against the use of hormone replacement therapy. 'Frightening females is fun,' she wrote in *The Age*. 'Women were frightened into using hormone replacement therapy by dire predictions of crumbling bones, heart disease, loss of libido, depression, despair, disease and death if they let nature take its course.' She argues that scaring women is 'big business and hugely profitable'. It is fear, she wrote, that 'makes women comply with schemes and policies that work against their interest' (EC).

**Ruth Picardie (1998) *Before I Say Goodbye*. Penguin.**
Ruth Picardie died in 1997. In the months before her death she wrote a regular column for *Observer Life*. This little book contains these writings. On their own these would not have been enough to fill a book so included with them are the emails that Ruth wrote to her friends during this time, their replies and also emails from many of her readers – people who had never met Ruth but were moved, often to tears, by her 'disarming candour' and 'mordant wit'. Matt Seaton, her husband, used these phrases in his 'After Words' which describe beautifully how Ruth expresses herself and her approach to having a terminal illness. This is a book that can help anyone, at any age, learn about death and what it is like to be facing death. It is touching and funny in equal measures on quite a difficult subject (EC).

**Jane Plant and Gill Tidey (2003) *Understanding, Preventing and Overcoming Osteoporosis*. Virgin Books.**
This is a well-researched and easy-to-read book that explains osteoporosis: testing for it, diagnosis, prevention and treatment. It also contains a recipe section (EC).

**Dorothy Rowe (1983) *Depression – the way out of your prison*. Routledge.**
This book is now in its third edition and is invaluable for anyone who suffers from depression or knows someone who does. It makes such good sense and makes fascinating reading (EC).

**Stephanie Wienrich and Josephone Speyer (2003) *The Natural Death Handbook*. London: The Natural Death Centre, 6 Blackstock Mews, Blackstock Road, London N4 2BT.**
Especially helpful about how to make practical and other arrangements (CL).

## 5 Biographies and autobiographies

Kate Adie (2002) *The Kindness of Strangers*. Headline.

John Bailey (1998) *Iris, A memoir*. Abacus.

Joan Bakewell (2003) *The Centre of the Bed*. Hodder & Stoughton
  (NB: In 2008 when this book was written Joan Bakewell was appointed a
  voice for the elderly by the UK Government.)

Alan Bennett (1994) *Writing Home*. Faber & Faber.

Alan Bennett (2005) *Untold Stories*. Faber & Faber.

Betty Boothroyd (2002) *Betty Boothroyd, the autobiography*. Random
  House/Arrow.

Bill Clinton (2004) *My Life*. Knopf Publishing Group/Random House.

Sheila Hancock (2008) *Just Me*. Bloomsbury.

Doris Lessing (1994) *Under My Skin, Volume one of my autobiography to
  1949*. HarperCollins.

Doris Lessing (1997) *Walking in the Shade, Volume two of my autobiography
  1949 to 1962*. HarperCollins.

Humphrey Lyttelton (2006) *It just Occurred to Me … The reminiscences and
  thoughts of Chairman Humph*. Robson Books.

Nelson Mandela (1994) *Long Walk to Freedom*. Little Brown.

Frank McCourt (2005) *Teacher Man*. HarperCollins.

John Miller (2004) *Darling Judi: A celebration of Judi Dench*. Weidenfeld &
  Nicolson.

Esther Rantzen (2001) *Esther – The autobiography*. BBC Books.

John Sergeant (2001) *Give Me Ten Seconds*. Macmillan.


## 6 Films on the theme of ageing

*About Schmidt* (2002)
*Away From Her* (2006)
*Cocoon* (1985)
*Driving Miss Daisy* (1989)
*Innocence* (2000)
*Iris* (2001)
*On Golden Pond* (1981)
*Shirley Valentine* (1989)
*The Straight Story* (1999)
*That's Life* (1986)
*Wild Strawberries* (1957)

## 7  Useful contacts

Age Concern Information Line
Tel: 0800 00 99 66
http://www.ageconcern.org.uk

Bloodaxe has a very good website where there is lots more detail on their books: http://www.bloodaxebooks.com/

Citizens Advice Bureau (CAB)
http://www.citizensadvice.org.uk

Discount-age.co.uk aims 'to put pressure on all sorts of organisations to get even better deals – and treatment – for the over 60s'. It lists a holiday company that offers walking in Spain and does not charge a single supplement. It seems it has just been developed to meet our needs:
http://www.discount-age.co.uk

and one of this website's founders, Valerie Singleton, also has a page devoted to spending wisely:
http://www.thisismoney.co.uk

Joseph Rowntree Foundation since 2000 has supported a research programme on how people are making transitions in work and towards retirement after age 50. They have funded 12 studies. Not all of it is relevant to us, but there is a list of publications. Joseph Rowntree Foundation Charitable Trust home page:
www.jrct.org.uk

National Union of Teachers
http://www.teachers.org.uk/

Open College of the Arts
Tel: 0800 731 2116
http://www.oca-uk.com

Reach – matching the skills of experienced people to the needs of voluntary organizations:
http://www.reach-online.org.uk/

SAGA, offers a range of options to the over fifties:
http://www.saga.co.uk

Samaritans, volunteer recruitment:
Tel: 08705 62 72 82

or follow the volunteering options from the main home page:
www.samaritans.org

State Pension
http://www.direct.gov.uk

Teachers' Pensions
http://www.teachersretirementagency.co.uk

The Dove ProAge campaign
Tel: 0800 085 1548
http://www.dove.co.uk

The University of the Third Age
Tel: 020 8466 6139
http://www.u3a.org.uk

University and College Union (UCU)
http://www.ucu.org.uk/

University Superannuation Scheme (USS)
http://www.usshq.co.uk/